ANGLING MEMORIES

ANGLING MEMORIES

by
Tag Barnes

Foreword by
Martin James

SPELLMOUNT LTD
Staplehurst

British Library Cataloguing in Publication Data:
A catalogue record for this book is available
from the British Library

Copyright © Tag Barnes 1994

ISBN 1-873376-23-5

First published in the UK in 1994 by
Spellmount Limited
The Old Rectory
Staplehurst
Kent TN12 0AZ

1 3 5 7 9 8 6 4 2

Typeset in Palatino by
Vitaset, Paddock Wood, Kent

Printed in Great Britain by
Ipswich Book Company Ltd.

CONTENTS

DEDICATION

To my wife Eileen, son Richard and daughter Vanessa
who were deprived of my company for many weekends
and weeks while I was away fishing.

FOREWORD

I do not believe there is an angler living who does not like to reminisce about his or her fishing. We all like to recall the good days – and the bad!

Anglers are great talkers and writers: it's no co-incidence that more books are published on angling than any other sport. In the 1950s angling was given a shot in the arm with the publication of *Angling Times* in July 1953. Suddenly the sport was free of its shackles – no longer did we fish as our grandfathers had. New names were showing us how to catch big fish by design and not luck.

This new breed of angling writer was led by a tall, good looking, silver haired, educated man named Richard Walker. He was joined by like minded men and one such was Yorkshire born Tag Barnes, who through the war years had been a commando of green beret fame who had seen action in North Africa, the Middle East and the Far East, including the infamous Burma jungle.

Tag, on his return to Yorkshire, turned once more to his twin loves of fishing and bird watching but, missing the action of the commando days, sought out the catching of specimen fish for his excitement, with great success. Tag was not a one fish man, he caught all sorts of coarse fish as well as some very big trout.

The writings from the pen of Tag Barnes in the 1950s and 1960s excited those like myself, who were desperate and thirsty for angling knowledge. He has given us books on angling, wildlife and his days as a commando. Now we have Angling Memories, a book that takes us back over Tag's lifetime. We meet his angling friends and waterside companions, on the way we smell the water mint, enjoy the dawns and the ducks, sample pastures new and catch a few fish.

Go and sit in your favourite chair, have a glass of wine and immerse yourself in Angling Memories, by a man who has given us so much over the years. Without men or women like Tag Barnes during the war years I would not be penning this foreword.

Martin James

7

INTRODUCTION

This is not a book about tremendous fish catches but more about a restless angler who learned some of the secrets of catching fish that are above average in weight. Had I been a more single minded angler, devoted to the pursuit of just one species, then there might well have been some larger individual fish to have been reported.

The book records the dedication of an angler to explore and enquire into the 'unknown'; to ignore much of the angling dogma that had been previously written and to relate new ideas that were discovered and developed, mostly after the last war. There are extracts in the book from several angling journals which are no longer with us. Older anglers may well remember the *Fishing Gazette*, *Angling*, *Fishing*, *Midland Angler* and *Angling Telegraph*. There are also extracts from present day newspapers and magazines such as *Angling Times*, *Anglers World* and *Coarse Angler*. My appreciation goes to the editors of these latter journals for allowing me to use some of the material that was published by them, and especially to Tim Paisley for his permission to use two extracts from *Carp Fisher*.

My thanks must also go to the following friends for the use of their photographs: Arthur Oglesby, Roy Shaw, Kevin Roberts, Brian Thompson, Fred J. Taylor and Ron Clay.

In the book there are big fish and fish catches that today would barely raise an eyebrow, but in the fifties, sixties and seventies would have set the blood stirring. I hope the reader will enjoy the reading of it as much as I have enjoyed the writing.

During the thirty or so years of the fifties, sixties and seventies I became involved in other activities that were a spin-off from actual fishing. I ran several angling night school classes for the education authorities of both Yorkshire and Derbyshire, and although they recompensed my efforts the remuneration was very meagre. In fact most 'after scene' activities were done at the time for the 'love of the game'.

There were many occasions when I was invited to angling clubs to present prizes, or to give a talk on specimen hunting or to take part in an angling quiz. They were all enjoyable, but they all meant evening trips after work and after most events I was financially out of pocket. Sometimes one would be offered petrol money . . . sometimes just a glass of beer. I recall after a prize giving session at a miners' welfare club being given a brace of rabbits which 'had only been caught that morning'!

The sixties were particularly hectic in so much that apart from some pretty intensive fishing I was involved in writing a weekly column, which went on for 11 years, for the *South Yorkshire Times*; a fortnightly piece for *Anglers Mail* and a monthly article for the *Midland Angler* and the *Angling Telegraph*. During that same decade I did a series of fishing pieces for Yorkshire Television and one for Tyne Tees called 'Go Fishing'.

As well as the aforementioned prize givings, lectures etc I wrote three books on angling and one on birds. It was around this time that I approached the Sheffield firm of Sportex Fishing Tackle and enquired if I might design a carp rod out of hollow fibre glass. I was given *carte blanche* to the rod blank room and was also introduced to the German representative of the blank manufacturers who was only too eager to supply me with any dimension of blank I desired. The resultant 'Tag Barnes Carp Rod' sold many hundreds and was used not only for carp fishing but as a salmon or pike rod. Testimonies arrived at Sportex showing photographs of all three species of fish in excess of thirty pounds being landed on the rod.

Six months after the appearance of the rod I gave up my job as a landscape gardener and joined the fishing tackle industry, where I remained until my retirement, and went on to design several other specialist rods including one for barbel, one for pike and one for general coarse fishing.

It was during the sixties that I became secretary of both the Cormorants Angling Club and the East Riding Specimen Group. Life was pleasantly chaotic!

THE EARLY DAYS

It all began I suppose when I was eight years old. My appetite had been whetted two years earlier when my father and two uncles took me along with them to Underbank reservoir just outside Sheffield. While they fished for roach I was given a length of spare line with lead and hook attached. A large worm was impaled and this was flung out into the reservoir with the other end of the line fastened to some secure object on the bank.

I would then wander off collecting mushrooms, blackberries, birds eggs or whatever was in season at the time, returning occasionally to check my 'tackle'. I shall always remember the excitement on seeing the line stretched taut and not hanging limply as I had left it, for I would know there was a trout on the end. On one occasion I 'caught' the best fish of the day, a fine brown trout of just under two pounds.

My lifelong interest in birds began by collecting their eggs – something I would condemn today, apart from the fact that it is illegal. I was encouraged by an uncle who was a good countryman and by the time I was called to war in 1939 I had a collection of over one hundred British birds eggs, of which I was very proud.

My father made me a large case with a lift-up glass lid and the eggs nestled inside on cotton wool, all nicely labelled. Tragedy struck during the war when the case, which had been stored on top of a wardrobe, was disloged and all the contents smashed! I still have not recovered from the shock. Whenever I came on leave I would lift down the case and sit and recall from where every egg was taken; how I waded out waste deep in a weedy pond for a little grebe's egg, and the time I had climbed a fifty foot high pine tree to add a sparrowhawk's to my collection. Or the time I had risked life and limb to reach a jackdaw's nest high up on a rock face. I remember my uncle telling me he had heard a woodlark singing – a scarce bird around Sheffield – and how we tracked down the nest and removed one egg from the four that were laid, and later how we saw the three remaining hatch out safely.

On my eighth birthday I was bought a rod. It was a three-piece, ten feet in length with the bottom two sections made from Spanish reed and the top piece from lance wood. It was 'christened' on the Chesterfield canal at a place called Ranby, near Retford, in Nottinghamshire. From home it was a round trip of about sixty miles and my father's return ticket on the bus cost one and sixpence (7½p), while I travelled at half price.

I recall the hours we spent there together with great affection. After disembarking from the bus we would walk along the towpath for nearly two miles to a favourite spot and here we would catch roach, perch, small chub and occasionally a tiny pike.

The tranquility of the place is etched in my mind forever. My interest in birds was widened and I saw my first nuthatch, yellow and pied wagtails and also sand martins which were nesting in a high sandy bank opposite. As well as catching fish I added to my collection the eggs of partridge, moorhen, skylark and long tailed tit.

Twice a day we had to move our tackle away from the towpath while a horse pulling a barge plodded past. At lunchtime I was sent along to a cottage two hundred yards away where a nice old lady made us a jug of hot sweet tea for which she charged two pence. Apart from the bargee and the old lady we saw no one else until we re-boarded the bus in the evening.

Over the years we explored many other stretches of this canal and local rivers, but my thoughts always return with profound feelings towards this particular stretch at Ranby. Whenever I think of my father it is not on the banks of the Trent, Witham or Welland, not at the side of the Huntspill, Soar, Wharf or any of the many other waterways we fished, but on the bank of that quiet canal where all my memories are of long sunny days filled with bird song.

Five other male members of my family were all match anglers and it is not surprising that I should copy their style and follow in their footsteps. At nine years old I was entered into a local pub match for youngsters. It had an upper age limit of eighteen, and 82 of us travelled by coaches to fish in a five hour match on a canal at Ambergate in Derbyshire.

Parents were allowed to sit by younger participants to advise, but not to assist in any way. It was a bright, hot sunny day and these conditions, combined with a lot of bankside activity, did not auger well for fishing. After four hours I had caught just three tiny roach and I was feeling somewhat dejected when my father, who had been on a reconnaissance, returned with the news that out of the other 81 competitors only four had keepnets in the water.

In the last ten minutes of the match I caught another tiny roach which brought my final weight of fish to 6½ ounces. The winner, an eighteen-year-old youth, had one fish which weighed half a pound and this pushed me into second place. At the prize giving a week later in an upstairs room of the pub, I remember even now my father beaming with pride as I went forward to collect my award.

Until the start of the war I fished whenever and wherever I could. The community centre on the estate where I lived ran an angling knockout competition on a local pond. The trial matches were held each weekday evening when the first three would go through to the final, which was fished on the Sunday morning. My father and I fished on different evenings so that we would not be competing against each other and for years we were always in the fish-off on the Sunday. We each won the final on only one occasion, but we were never out of the first half dozen.

THE WAR YEARS

This fishing malady continued until the outbreak of war. I had joined the Territorial Army in the summer of 1939 and was called up the day before war started. Being still only seventeen, I and several others were considered too young to be sent abroad and were posted to Norfolk where we joined an artillery regiment.

It wasn't long before I sent for my fishing tackle and whenever time allowed I explored the local waters around the camp. I discovered a quiet lake not far away in the middle of a wood and it was here I caught my first tench and saw my first bittern.

A later move into Huntingdonshire brought further waters to search out. The Great Ouse and several lakes were fished and from the river I caught my first big pike. It was the largest fish I had ever seen and although I didn't realise it at the time I suppose I was indoctrinated with the bug of specimen hunting. It was given away to a local publican.

The tackle I assembled for the latter was extremely crude. The rod, which I bought locally, was as stiff as a poker and in retrospect, would have been more suitable for tunny fishing. The big wooden centre-pin reel was loaded with thick cuttyhunk line, strong enough to have held a horse!

I also caught a large carp and the memory of its capture still makes me blush! I had been poaching rabbits on a nearby private estate not far from the camp and had noticed several huge fish wallowing on the surface of a lake. I had no idea what they were but I returned at first light one morning to find two of them still cruising around with their large dorsal fins breaking the surface.

I was armed with my pike tackle, except that in place of a roach livebait I pushed the eye of the treble through a large lump of crust and attached it to the cuttyhunk. Although I had never seen one I suspected the fish were carp and I realised it would require some strong tackle to get one out and on to dry land. Several yards of line were pulled from the reel, but the first cast I made fell short into a bed of weeds. The three points of the treble held the crust securely and my second attempt landed it in open water.

The whole episode was temendously exciting. Added to the fact that I was poaching I could hardly bare the strain when one of these leviathans moved sedately over to the crust and sucked it in. I struck hard, wound and ran backwards as fast as I could. The commotion was unbelievable as the fish thrashed its way through the weedbed, but in seconds I had it lying on the bank. I wasn't ashamed at the time (I feel very guilty now!) but I killed the fish and carried it back to camp, where some of it was eaten.

What I remember most vividly was not so much the excitement of the capture, but the nightmarish trip I had back to base trying not to be observed and struggling with the fish and my gear under two barbed wire fences, over a couple of five barred gates and across a main road!

It is not a fish I have talked about much – my shame grew as the years went by!

My excuse for such a dastardly deed is that there was a war going on, and some strange things happen during wars! I hope I am forgiven!

In 1942 I volunteered to join the Army Commandos and for eight weeks was stationed at Achnacarry in Scotland, where I did my initial training. There was little time for fishing, but I did manage to borrow some tackle from a local stalker and caught my first seatrout on a worm trundled along the bottom of a nearby river. It wasn't a monster, barely 2lbs, but it gave me a taste of the fighting power of these fish. While there I saw both my first black and red throated divers, my first black grouse and a memorable golden eagle.

There was not much time for angling when I was posted to join No 1 Commando until much later when I managed a few hours fishing on a small lake near Tabarka in North Africa. I caught some fish which I thought were chub, at least they looked like chub in shape, but in 'colour' appeared to be more silver than bronze. In Egypt I managed a short spell fishing in the Mediterranean and caught some highly coloured tropical looking fish which I returned alive to the water.

When my Commando unit arrived in India I discovered my rod had somehow been lost in transit. We were stationed under canvas in a camp not far from Poona and on my first short leave I found a shop that sold odds and ends of fishing tackle. I bought a six foot, two piece rod made from split bamboo and several other items such as line, floats, hooks and lead weights.

There was no opportunity to fish until we became involved in jungle training at a place called Belgaum in Southern India. Not far from the camp was a small but fast flowing river which consisted of long, swift glides interspersed with the occasional pool.

The biggest problem was in getting to the bankside which was heavily overgrown, but after several attempts I managed to hack my way through with a machete. I had not seen any sign of fish movement and was not sure how to tackle the job when I finally arrived. A size 10 eyed hook was baited with a paste made from bread and corned beef, and I cast this out with a coffin lead fixed about twelve inches from the hook.

From time to time I flicked in a few pieces of loose bait and periodically rebaited the hook. I am not sure how long I sat there but quite suddenly, without any warning, the rod was almost snatched from my hand and I found myself struggling with a very strong fish which more or less did as it liked for what seemed hours.

Eventually a very exhausted fish rolled on its side and I lifted it out by hand. At the time I knew nothing about 'foreign' fish and examined what looked very much like a barbel of around five pounds. I now realise that what I had caught was a small mahseer.

Whenever I had the chance I would sit beside that pool using the same bait but I never had another bite. In retrospect I would probably have been wiser to have tried a spoon bait of some description.

A few weeks later when on manoeuvre, several miles downstream on the same river, we exploded some plastic explosive in a much larger pool than the one I had fished. When the waves subsided a dozen or more fish floundered on the surface and we dragged them ashore to take back to camp. Three of them were quite enormous and I remember as we carried them, threaded on bamboo poles, that their tails touched the ground.

My only other session of note in India was much later when on leave, 9,000 feet up in the blue mountains at a place called Ootacumund. I went with two good pals,

George Westly and Arthur Barnett, and while there we organised a three day fishing trip to a remote trout stream called the Pycara.

The tackle was loaned and the trip booked through a game hunting establishment. After loading a taxi with everything we needed, including a supply of gin and whisky, we left with a *shikari* – an Indian guide – and travelled along some rough roads until we could go no further.

The rest of the journey was covered on foot until eventually we arrived at a 'Dak' bungalow which was tucked away among some trees by the side of a most attractive river. The bungalow was strictly a shooting lodge used by people hunting leopard or tiger and although sparsely furnished was more than adequate for our purpose.

In our contract the *shikari* was to tend all our needs, which he did admirably. He prepared all our meals, dug our bait and had a good log fire burning on our return from fishing. The nights were chilly and after dinner we would sit by the fire sipping gin and yarning until ready for bed.

We had gone to fish for trout and the first evening found us float fishing worms in one of the many pools along the river. Although we caught a few trout we were completely taken aback when we began catching carp, having no idea there were any in the river. There was a mixture of mirror and fully scaled fish weighing up to around three pounds. They provided some tremendous sport on the light tackle we were using, and we killed a few which the *shikari* dished up in a delicious meal. We spent more time trying to catch them in preference to trout and I must say those great little fighters gave me a love of carp which was to last me for the rest of my life.

Many years after the war I met Ken Mansfield, the then editor of the monthly magazine *Angling* (now no more). He had also fished the Pykara on several occasions and he told me that originally it was purely a trout water until someone experimented by introducing a few carp which, although they never grew big, evantually spawned and finally took over the river.

My fishing in Ceylon (now called Sri Lanka) began on a quayside where some big 'bluefish' were swimming, ten feet down in and out of some wooden pilings. I hooked half a dozen but only managed to land one of about 3lbs. The rest dropped off as I tried to lift them out from the depths.

16

They had a definite bluish tint and looked like big fat 'blue' chub. Some of them must have weighed at least eight pounds.

In Ceylon the unit was stationed in *bashas* on the beach at Trincomalee. We launched into a hard training schedule but on the occasional day off I would set out with my tackle to explore the surrounding countryside and, not far from camp, I discovered a large lagoon. It was in a beautiful setting and abounded with birds, but it became terribly frustrating not being able to name them. Some I did recognise after seeing mounted specimens in the Bombay Natural History Museum, but I would have given a lot to have had one of today's modern bird identification handbooks.

I circled the lagoon, which appeared to have extensive shallows, until I came across a fallen tree which leaned out over the water. Scrambling as far along it as I could I lowered my float tackle into what was obviously deeper water.

My bait was the usual paste and bully beef mix and after about ten minutes the little porcupine quill I was using began to bob before finally dipping below the surface. The plump half pound fish I hauled up looked for all the world like a roach and, with a view to a change of diet, I killed it and threw it over my shoulder to the bank.

After catching half a dozen I noticed a bird, which I now know was a Brahmini kite, flying away with a fish in its talons. I glanced back and realised that several of my catch had disappeared! I caught a few more, keeping a wary eye open for the kite, and returned to camp with half a dozen fish that made good eating after being cooked by Arthur who, at the time, was in charge of the cookhouse.

On another trip, further round the lagoon, I found a deeper spot close in to the bank from where I caught some more 'roach' and again they made a nice change of diet. One day I caught a fish which caused some alarm both to me and a passing native who had stopped to watch me fishing. Looking back now I realise it was some sort of sunfish. After carefully hauling it from the water and on to the bank it proceeded to blow itself up to about the size of a football. It was covered in sharp spines and made a squeaking noise and before I could do anything further the native, who by now was quite excited and was repeatedly shouting 'bo-crab', (which means in English, I think, 'very bad') grabbed a stick and killed it.

There was one other strange thing about this fish. Its teeth were not needle-like, as one might find in a pike or trout, but were like the teeth of a young child and when I tapped them with a pencil they were quite solid.

After Ceylon I did not get a chance to fish anymore until we reached Burma, and here there was little time for anything except to battle with the Japanese. There was time enough, however, for one session in a jungle stream pool. It was no more than eight feet in diameter but from it I caught a dozen small, perch-like fish that had faint horizontal stripes instead of vertical.

Fishing in Burma was curtailed after I was wounded until, after convalescing, I went on leave to the aforementioned Ootacumund. I was still in India when the war finally ended and was moved with my unit to Hong Kong to act as occupational troops. Fishing time was limited although I did manage to fish off the coast, but caught only crabs and dogfish.

Just before Christmas in 1945, along with a few more troops, I was detailed to take some prisoners of war back home to Japan. I went ashore at Kagoshima and Sasebo in the South islands but could not find any suitable fresh water in which to fish, so I contented myself by fishing off either the dockside or the ship where I caught nothing more exotic than more dogfish.

This then virtually ended my wartime fishing exploits. I did fish abroad again after the war in Cyprus, the Balearic islands, Israel and Spain, but these were trips involving some serious bird watching and the fishing was a distinctly subsidiary activity.

RETURN TO PEACETIME

Re-settling in peacetime brought a resumption of angling, much of it in casual pleasure fishing with the occasional competition thrown in. I organised a rather unique annual match between six male members of my family, all with the same surname of Barnes. Match day was the only time all six of us met and there was great competition between us.

I was appointed secretary and an uncle treasurer. A small monthly contribution from us all covered our expenses on *the* day. At first we chose venues which could be reached by train but after three years we hired a mini-bus which was driven by a teetotal friend. This allowed us to stop off on the way back to celebrate without having the worry of driving home afterwards!

We bought a cup and had it engraved 'The Barnes Trophy' which the winner held for twelve months and, also, each season we took turns to pick the venue.

One amusing incident occurred on one of the earlier outings when we set off by train to fish the Derbyshire Derwent at a place called Duffield. We had been travelling 10 minutes when an inspector entered our compartment. After checking our tickets he stared at us long and hard. Finally he said, 'You have got a treble up.' He continued, 'You are smoking in a non-smoking carriage; you are sitting in a first class compartment with second class tickets and, thirdly, you are on the wrong train!'

The train did not stop at Duffield but carried on to Derby where we had to disembark and catch a bus back to our destination! The matches came to an end after the fourth member of the family passed away. It wasn't much fun just fishing against my cousin Frank!

But throughout this period of time my leanings were more and more directed towards the catching of specimen fish. Matches were finally discarded in favour of pleasure fishing after better quality fish.

It was in 1947 when fishing a private lake that I received my first lesson, when I came to realise that it wasn't possible to combine the two worlds of match fishing and the catching of big fish and be successful at both. It had to be one or the other and this outing became my day of decision.

It was a heavily weeded water containing a rich amount of natural food and a variety of fish to satisfy any angler. I spent many happy hours there, fishing between the lily beds and filling my keepnet with a mixture of roach, bream, perch, rudd and the inevitable jack pike – all caught on maggots fished on small hooks dubbed to fine gut-lengths. Several fish were lost in the lilies but this was taken as a matter of course without causing much unnecessary heartache or lasting concern.

On the day which left its permanent mark I had ground-baited a clear shallow swim before dawn. When the light brightened enough for me to see the bottom I saw something which held me spellbound. A shoal of bream was filtering out from beneath the nearby lilies and feeding on my groundbait.

The majority of these fish were frighteningly large. I caught what was probably the smallest which weighed 5lb, but then the nightmare began. I was devastatingly smashed at least a dozen times as these monster fish picked up my bait and moved nonchalantly off with it into the lilies. I hadn't any hooks with me larger than the size 16 I was using, so when the last one went I had just to call it a day.

My subsequent visits, properly armed with more substantial tackle, never produced another bite, in fact the queer twist to this story is that I never saw those bream again except a dead one I found by the side of the lake. It weighed 11½lb.

BIG FISH HUNTING

My serious initiation into the world of specimen hunting developed alongside my participation in angling journalism. As ideas were spawned they were passed on through various publications to be tested, enlarged upon and discussed. If they were of use to anyone then I was delighted.

I never concentrated on catching one species to the exclusion of all others, although some were given my individual attention that sometimes spanned two to three years. As a result of this and depending on what I was fishing for at the time I was often quoted by the angling press as being a carp or pike specialist; a grayling or chub expert; a roach or dace fanatic, etc. I was none of these.

I enjoyed fishing for all species and I was more successful with some than others, but after forty or so years I have reached most of the targets I set for myself. Some I exceeded but there were some I didn't reach, but who knows! I once gave myself a task of catching a five pound chub from the river Swale in Yorkshire and for eight consecutive years I caught at least one a few ounces either side of that weight, and I was more than satisfied. But my best chub from the upper Great Ouse was exactly one pound heavier, so my cup was more than full.

By the same token I yearned to catch a three pound grayling but have only managed two fish, both of which weighed 2½lb. The main reason for my failure was perhaps that I never fished a water that held any, or hardly any, fish of this size.

My twenty pound pike target was reached, but I have lost count of the double figure fish which provided me with a lot of joy.

My carp catches have followed on similar lines as my pike results – something that would be sneezed at today, but during the fifties and sixties big carp (any carp!), especially in my part of the world, were very thin on the ground. I suppose my best achievement was during the fifties when I became the first angler to catch four doubles in one night, especially as this was in Yorkshire!

It would have been nice to have topped thirty with both of the afore-mentioned species, but it causes me no grief. I would much rather have caught a three pound grayling!

I had a barbel approaching double figures, but pride of place, in my mind, must go to a fish weighing 8½lb from the Swale. Several tench over the magic 5lb mark have rolled in (they were big in the fifties!) but my six pounder eluded me by two ounces.

I would have loved a double figure bream but I am reasonably content with a best of 6lb 12oz. I am happy with a perch over three pounds, but I wish I hadn't caught it when I was pike fishing! Crucians, roach and rudd have all topped the two pound mark and one dace over the magical 1lb (on fly), but plenty around the 12-14oz range. My best (unwanted) eel weighed 4½lb. I have never fished for Zander in my life!

As I have already mentioned, carp fishing in the North of the country in the fifties was very sparse – it is not prolific even now – and it was towards the middle of the decade that I met up with the Thompson brothers, Wilf and Brian. They told me of a carp water they had found at Wortley, a village not far from Sheffield.

The lake was in the grounds of Wortley Hall and permission to fish was granted for a ridiculously small sum. As well as carp the water held a head of tench and we spent many days, and nights, in the pursuit of both. There were about a dozen people fishing the water who were all of like mind in the catching of big fish, and it was decided that we would form a group which we named the Cormorants Angling Club. It was possibly the first formation of anglers in Britain who were solely devoted to specimen hunting. We held monthly meetings and exchanged ideas and we organised outings to various parts of the country with the sole aim of catching big fish.

All progressed well until one day we received the news that the lake at Wortley, due to mining subsidence below, would have to be drained. The owners agreed that if we could find another home for the fish then we could take all we could catch. I paid a visit to John Hollingworth, the then estate agent of Sir Osbert Sitwell, who offered us a half acre water called Slittingmill pond for a nominal rent.

We met quickly and drew up plans as to how the fish were to be transferred. As most of the fishing would be taking place after work, and as my house was about half-way between Wortley and Slittingmill, it was decided that any fish caught could be left overnight in our bath (!) and then moved on the following evening to their new home.

In retrospect I suppose it was all rather amusing. At the time my wife, Eileen, was in bed immobilised with an attack of lumbago. For ten days I dared not go to bed until 2am in case someone turned up with some fish. On a good night the bath would be heaving with mainly tench but also carp to 12½lb in weight. And then, after the fish were settled in, we would retire to the bedroom where my wife would patiently listen while coffee was drunk and tales were told of the evening's scoop.

Although small, the pond at Slittingmill was interesting in so much that it was once a section of the nearby polluted river Rother. Our particular length was blocked off during the construction of an adjacent railway bridge.

We spent a lot of time at the pond on organised working parties; digging, repairing fences, putting up barbed wire and erecting a new gate. During the dragging we discovered there was a good head of the uncommon crested newt present and other smaller acquatic life was also there in abundance.

We widened our horizons and rented a lovely two mile stretch of the river Idle in Nottinghamshire. It was a river I had dearly loved since I was a boy, and my father and I had caught from it some tremendous bags of excellent roach, for which it was famous. From time to time it was subjected to a mild pollution caused by coal washings from pits in the area, but it didn't have too detrimental an effect on the sport. One strange thing about the Idle was that it didn't respond very well to recognised big fish tactics. The primary species was roach and undoubtedly its better specimens were caught on either float-trotted maggot or caster.

The chub present never ran to very large sizes but even these were better fished for using the same method one would use for roach. My best fish, which weighed just a fraction under five pounds came to two casters fished on a size 16 hook and float tackle.

Disaster struck Slittingmill pond twice after only a few years fishing. The first came one severe winter when the lake was covered for several weeks in thick ice. When the thaw finally came we found our losses were not as bad as we had anticipated. A few carp were lost but not sufficient to prevent us carrying out a further restock.

The second and final blow came the following year when rain fell heavily for days on end. The whole of the area was flooded and the nearby river Rother overflowed its banks and covered the pond with four feet of polluted water. Alas, when the water subsided we discovered an almost hundred percent wipe-out and we agreed unanimously to give up our lease. The club became fragmented and after a while was finally disbanded.

Shortly after the demise of the Cormorants the Northern Specimen Hunters Group was formed and such stalwarts as Eric Hodgson, Ron Clay, Dick Clegg, John Neville, Ray Webb and Reg Brotherton ensured that new ideas kept the club on its toes and forever forward looking.

From this point onwards the book reveals some of the many outings, facts and theories that I put forward during the fifties, sixties and seventies. Many of the trips described are with friends and at other times when fishing on my own. I trust some of my memories will be enjoyed by present day 'modern' anglers and beginners alike.

CARP – 1950-1970

To round off one carp season, Reg Brotherton and I fished a two acre pool in North Yorkshire. The place was private and the owner of the water, in order to deter would-be trespassers, allowed the banks to run completely wild. Even the few fishable swims were heavily overgrown with bushes and trees and I'm sure that only the hunter of specimens would consider them fishable.

We arrived late Saturday afternoon and, after a 'recce' round the water, settled for two swims that were about 80 yards apart and separated by a veritable jungle. Most of the trees on the banks had branches stretching out over the pool and it was beneath one of these that Reg, fishing near the deep end, drifted a piece of floating crust. Within half an hour of starting to fish this crust was taken, and after a good scrap I had the pleasure of lifting out Reg's fish – a splendid mirror carp of exacty 13lb.

After this excellent start I left most of my gear at a pitch halfway along the pond, where I intended to spend the night, and made my way quietly along to the shallows armed with rod, landing net and bait. I couldn't see any carp, but with care managed to get out a piece of crust between the branches. For fully twenty minutes in the closing darkness I sat behind cover, keeping a careful eye on my bait, when quite suddenly a carp appeared and without a moment's hesitation swam up to the crust and engulfed it. The ensuing commotion made by the fish as I held it on a tight line (there was little room for fancy playing) brought Reg along and in a short time I had the pleasure of returning the compliment by letting him slip the net under a 10½ pounder.

Our cups were full. If we didn't have another bite we were satisfied. But it wasn't to be – at least not for me. Reg's glory was, in fact, crowded into that first half hour, for he never had any further runs. For me, however, the night was only just beginning.

I settled down in my swim with flake on one rod and paste on a second. At about 10.30pm my buzzer sounded and its red eye blinked agitatedly as the carp moved off in a steady run. I hooked this fish and we slugged it out together by the pale light of a 'little' moon. First a 'boil' somewhere out in the pond centre, and then a hissing of line through the water as the fish 'kited' in for the branches on a long line. Quick winding and some heavy sidestrain prevented the fish from reaching this snag and then the clutch 'burred' as the carp shot out and 'boiled' a second time way out in the middle. Not wishing to fetch Reg from his rods (or bring him along the tree-tangled bank in the darkness) I netted the fish myself – a second fine mirror that weighed 13lb 12oz.

Before midnight I had repeated the procedure, this time netting a fully scaled fish of 13lb 4oz. By 3am the moon had disappeared behind heavy clouds and at this time, in the inky blackness, the bite alarm sounded a third time. This was a heavier fish and, after some minutes had passed without it weakening, I decided to call Reg to assist with the netting. But before he had risen from his seat the fish had shed the hook and I was left ruminating as to why!

Nothing further happened until just before dawn when again the bait was taken and my, by this time, cramped muscles were forced into action. This fish took almost ten minutes to subdue and proved to be the best and last fish of the trip – another mirror of 15½lb which, with Reg's thirteen pounder, made a total weight of 66lb of carp during our one-night stand. My four fish turned out to be the first four double figure carp to be taken in one night. Today they wouldn't raise an eyebrow, but nearly forty years ago they were talked about for weeks!

'Jungle' carp

I am not sure whether it was Confuscius or Richard Walker who wrote: "Bait in trees no catchee fish". I am sure, however that this is not strictly true, as I discovered on an outing to a neighbouring club water. The previous season Reg Brotherton and I had made a visit to this lake, arriving after dark, and when it became light enough to see discovered that we had been fishing over a thick bed of filamentous algae – in which no doubt our baits had been buried. This time we arrived earlier and took along a drag.

We dumped our gear at a spot halfway between the shallows and the dam end, and before doing any more I crept along to the shallows and threw in about half a dozen pieces of crust.

The shallow end of this water is worth mentioning. At one time the lake must have been much smaller. From where a stream trickled in, and for almost a third of its length, were numerous dead trees standing upright and lifeless in the water. There were trees of all shapes and sizes, and snags galore where gales had blown many dead branches into the water. The whole place looked rather weird – somewhat like a prehistoric swamp forest. It was, as will be imagined, a haven for carp, but getting them out was quite a problem.

After rigging our tackle and dragging a swim, Reg and I returned to these shallows armed with carp gear and some crusts. We crept along, keeping low behind the marginal sedge, and as we carefully lobbed out our baits we noticed the loose crusts that I had previously introduced could no longer be seen.

About ten minutes had passed when I noticed a deep swirl beneath my bait, and the crust wobbled violently. Then quite suddenly, it just vanished, only to reappear again just as I was about to tighten. This happened two or three times until finally down went the crust, and as the line commenced to straighten on the surface I rose to my feet and drove home the hook. I will not describe the ensuing battle in detail except to say that it was a hectic one that required all my wits before Reg could eventually slip the net under 9lb, hard fighting mirror carp and lift it from its aquatic jungle.

We continued fishing the shallows until after midnight, using balanced paste and crust baits, but with no further success; after which we returned to our original dragged swims and baited up.

We put out two rods each – one baited with flake and the other with lobworms. At about 2am a big, almost full moon rose from behind the trees opposite making the whole place as bright as day. It was at this hour that we began to get a series of runs – short, half-hearted efforts that took a long time to develop. The reason for these 'awkward' bites became apparent as we started to catch fish – small rudd to a pound in weight on the flake baits, and tiny perch that had gorged themselves on the worms. Frustrating!

27

This state of affairs lasted throughout the moonlit hours, until after dawn in fact, and the prospects of catching another carp became more and more remote until eventually we decided to return home to discuss the antics of small fish that break the rules and feed in the moonlight! It is not unusual, of course, to catch other species when after carp at night – whatever the visibility – and sometimes good specimens are landed. But I have noticed that on a cloudless night with a big moon one often gets pestered with what would normally be described as daylight feeding species.

I have often thought, that on a water where these fish are of a good size, it might be interesting to scale down one's tackle and perhaps try for them exclusively sometimes when the moon is bright.

'Twin' carp

On the Friday evening of the first full weekend of a new season Reg and I made our way into North Yorkshire to try for carp. We had mixed feelings about the outlook. Naturally, on this first trip our spirits were high, but downpours of cold, heavy rain rather took the shine off things. However, we were quickly cheered to find on arrival at the lake that the water temperature was a very desirable 62°F and that a few carp were in evidence in the shallows.

With little more than an hour of daylight left, we quickly prepared ourselves for an all-night vigil and were soon settled in our favourite pitches, hopefully awaiting the first 'run' of the season. But by 8am the following morning, when we 'knocked off' to prepare breakfast and snatch a few hours sleep, our buzzers were still as silent as they had been throughout the night.

It was in fact a very short sleep because two hours later Reg roused me from my slumbers with a cup of tea to inform me that some fish were active under the branches of some overhanging trees on the opposite bank. It was also at this juncture that the rain started: at first a steady drizzle, then a downpour that was to continue throughout the day until dark. But, unperturbed, we gathered together the necessary gear and set off towards the far side of the lake.

En route to the shallows I spotted a carp and managed to put out a lump of paste without causing any apparent alarm.

Ten minutes later the line hanging from the rod tip began to straighten and I struck. There was a tremendous 'boil' in the water followed by a glimpse of a fat golden flank, then the fish shed the hook and was gone. I followed Reg's footprints in the wet grass feeling very despondent.

An hour after this episode, in a fresh pitch, I forgot my missed fish *and* the incessant rain as I watched the line slipping steadily from the spool. When the resultant strike connected with a good fish, I felt even better. I was fishing a 'tight' swim with sycamore boughs dripping into the water on either side, and I had quite a tussle before I netted a plump mirror which weighed 15lb.

We placed the fish in a keepnet and then ate a damp tea (it was still coming down in 'buckets') before returning to our respective swims. At about 9pm my line again started to run out confidently as a fish moved off with my paste, and the water showered from the rod as I drove in the hook. Reg netted this one, which turned out to be almost an identical twin to the first in that it was exactly the same weight.

By nightfall, having had more than enough of our English summer, we retired to my van to get some sleep; but before doing so we baited up one swim, having decided we would both fish it the following morning.

Four o'clock, with the light just tinting the eastern sky, found us back in position with our paste baits lying among the groundbait. But we got no further runs, and after a late breakfast we packed our gear and set off for home. We were weary but content, at least I was with two carp weighing 30lb, but I would have been even happier if Reg had caught one of them.

Carp and maggots – 1962

One of my most interesting outings in the year, despite the fact that larger fish were caught elsewhere on other trips, was a visit to a small pond that contained carp and tench. The carp here ran to about 15lb and the tench to around 5lb, with many fish ranging between half-a-pound and 3lb. This pond was, however, a problem water. Despite many well prepared plans by club members over three or four years, neither species had come to the net with any regularity.

Occasional fish had been taken by using the usual tactics – lobs and bread baits free-lined in the usual manner, or crust fished on the surface – but big bags were indeed rare.

The main hazard was probably the great depth of soft silt that covered the bottom and probably obscured most baits that were fished there. Combined paste and crust baits and a piece of crust on sliding link had been tried to overcome the problem, mostly to no avail.

After giving the problem much thought I arrived at the water one evening with a quantity of groundbait and a tinful of maggots. My first task was to run a drag through one of the existing swims, after which I moved to another spot where I fished until midnight without a bite. I returned to the dragged swim, deposited all my groundbait with a liberal dosage of maggots, and then retired to my sleeping bag.

By 4am I was out and prepared my tackle which consisted of a carp rod, six pound line and a No 8 eyed hook baited with six maggots. I had decided to use float tackle and rigged up a porcupine quill that two shots would sink out of sight. When the float was adjusted so that the lower shot rested on the bottom, the weight of the second shot pulled down the float until only a quarter-inch showed above the surface.

Ten minutes after starting to fish the float behaved exactly as I had hoped it would. A fish picked up the bait, the combined weight of the two shots took the float completely under, and I netted a small, fully scaled carp of 3lb. This was followed by a tench of similar proportions, and then a mirror carp of 2½lb.

To cut a long story short, by 8.30am I had in the net eight carp and four tench, all weighing between 2lb and 3lb. Two larger carp, one in double figures, came off when I tried to stop them reaching a bed of lilies.

The swim was full of bubbling fish that I continually fed with loose maggots, and they were obviously preoccupied with this bait. Both lobworm and bread, legered on a second rod and fished in the same swim, remained untouched the whole time I was fishing. The fish were still feeding at 8.30am when I finally ran out of hookbait, so I can only conjecture what the total bag might have been had I had more maggots.

The catch, except for this particular water, wasn't significant, but several facts emerged from the experiment. One is that the larger carp, as well as the small ones, were pre-pared to feed, and a stronger line plus a larger hook holding more maggots might have brought about their downfall. I couldn't wait to try out the method on a water where the fish were bigger!

More Carp on maggots

It wasn't until the last couple of hours that I suddenly realised how tired I really was. It had all begun five days earlier when I made my way north into Yorkshire ready for a five day session after carp. I reached the lake at around 3pm pitching the tent in torrential rain. With everything stowed away I made my way around the water's edge armed with a bush saw, lopping shears, spade and a weed drag.

The previous four days and nights of non-stop gales had littered parts of the lake with broken branches, most of which I managed to drag out, the saw and lopping shears being used to remove more offending boughs and branches from around various pitches.

At the top of the water a wall, which was built two years previously out of large stones and clay in order to divert part of a stream through the lake, had been washed away, apparently by a cloudburst in the surrounding hills. After two hours in the still pouring rain I had lifted enough stones and puddled enough clay to divert the stream once more through the lake.

As I made my way back to the bivouac area my guest for the next four days, Kevin Roberts, was just arriving. We had a meal, rigged our tackle, viewed the lake (without any sign of a carp) and then talked ourselves into a fever of anti-cipation until darkness began to fall.

Kevin had chosen himself a swim halfway along the lake while I chose a pitch in the shallows. At 2am with the tem-perature falling rapidly I moved my gear to a spot at the dam end, laced the swim heavily with maggots and crawled into the tent for a couple of hours' restless sleep. By the first light of a chilly dawn I was back at the swim, eager to try out the method I had used on the smaller carp pre-viously mentioned.

On one rod I fixed a lightly shotted float with one small shot resting on the bottom in seven feet of water. The hook was a size 8 tied direct to a 9lb line and baited with ten maggots. The second rod carried a free-lined potato and was attached to a bite alarm. I noticed a few bubbles in the maggot baited area and the float had barely settled when it gave a couple of bobs and disappeared. My strike resulted in a heavy plunge on the rod and after a brisk struggle I landed a nice mirror of 13lb.

Two hours later I repeated the performance, this time another mirror weighing 15lb. Two double figure carp before breakfast on this water was as much as anyone could ask. Kevin came round to see me land the second fish. He had fished out the night without a run, except from a small eel.

After a quick breakfast around 9am the fish were photographed and returned. I then telephoned the angling press with the information, returned to the lake and, after another session strengthening the stream diversion wall, slept for three hours.

At teatime Kevin appeared with the news that he had netted a 6lb fully scaled fish which had taken a piece of bread flake in the middle of the afternoon. To my great disappointment this was to be Kevin's one and only carp of the session. By 7pm we were back on the dam, Kevin fishing one end and me the other.

When it became too dark to see our floats we both legered maggots on one rod and potato on the second. Nothing stirred to either bait until about 1am when Kevin had a run on his maggot baited hook. This turned out to be a fat eel of about 2lb which managed to get its tail around a batch of weeds. Being the good host I offered to wade out with the net, forgetting I had earlier changed my thigh waders for gum boots! I retired to my sleeping bag with a wet right foot!

Three hours later we were back on the dam but lunchtime arrived without any sign of a carp. We spent the afternoon with saw and shears, in a steady drizzle, opening up an old swim which had completely overgrown.

That same evening I settled down once more in my swim on the dam. By this time the rain was coming down in sheets making it difficult to see the quarter inch of quill peeping above the surface. At around 8pm the float suddenly vanished and I was on my feet struggling with a heavy fish which bore deeply in a series of alarming plunges.

By the time Kevin arrived I was weighing a fat bellied mirror which pulled the scale to 23lb. Fifteen minutes after consigning the fish to a large sack which was sunk in the water I hit a second heavy fish which shed the hook on its first long run.

Quarter of an hour later the float dipped for the third time and on this occasion Kevin arrived in time to slip the net under yet another mirror weighing 17lb. I think it was at this point, as Kevin went to fetch his tackle round, that I heard him mutter something about beginning to hate the sight of me.

This was Friday evening and no further fish were caught. Kevin departed on Saturday afternoon and I fished well on into the night and, apart from a break to build up the over-flow from the lake, most of Sunday.

As I watched the tip of my quill in the fading light I felt tired, but I also felt a glow of contentment. Four double figure carp, with one of them over twenty from this diffi-cult water all caught up on the humble maggot was very satisfying.

More on Carp and maggots

After reporting catching carp on floatfished maggots I had numerous inquiries about the technique involved. Let me say straight away that catching carp using this method was not new at the time, but it was unusual. To most carp anglers floats are an anathema, baits being free lined or legered in some form or other. On most waters these proven methods are still probably the best for producing results.

However we are inclined to become bogged down by convention, which can be fatal. Thinking back over the years I realise that many of the successes I have had have been due to the fact that I have been *unconventional*. I have written before that adaptability plays a tremendous part in the role of a successful angler, be he coarse, game or sea fisherman. The leading anglers in any branch of the sport are adaptable, always on the look-out for a technique that will help keep them one jump ahead of the fish.

On one small lake I fished it is possibly true to say that I had caught every carp in it at least twice. When you add to this the fish my friends had caught plus the ones which had been pricked, hooked and lost then it was not surprising that these carp had become wary. The days of typical carp runs had virtually disappeared. Even with free offerings, carp could sometimes be observed just 'lipping' the bait.

Using a float for carp is something which had been nagging me for years, but while the occasional fish was being caught by normal methods, the idea was left in the back of my mind. Billy Lane once wrote that a float gives a quicker bite indication than any form of legering, and of course he was right. There are times, as we are all aware, when it would be impractical to use a float, but why not use one for carp when fishing during the hours of daylight?

Carp being the capricious feeders they are, means it is possible to sit over a bed of maggots for days without any sign of a fish, but the interesting thing is that once they *do* start to feed it is possible to take two or even three fish in a short period. The disturbance and upheaval of playing and netting one fish doesn't appear to upset any other carp which may be in the area, except when extremely shallow water is being fished. On one occasion I hooked three double figure fish all in the space of 30 minutes.

The beauty of it all is that with a float one can see exactly what is happening. On one visit to a favourite water I carried out an interesting experiment. I had cast a maggot-loaded hook into the shallows when suddenly I spotted a fish which looked as if it might make double figures, lying just below the surface, four yards from the float. I carefully threw it about half-a-dozen maggots and saw the fish swirl and take two. The next half-a-dozen were tossed in about a yard nearer the float. The fish moved forward, took another couple but remained near the surface.

I continued the process until the carp was about three feet from the float when I let go a mighty handful which dropped just behind the float in the baited area. The fish swirled, taking several maggots and then, as I had hoped, uptailed and followed the rest down. It wasn't a monstrous carp but at that moment I must admit feeling more than excited. When the float trembled I thought for a second that the fish was brushing against the nylon, but as it sailed away I struck and had a lively tussle with what turned out to be a fully scaled fish just a few ounces short of double figures. I reckoned I earned that carp by sheer cunning!

Floatfished maggots for carp will not be successful on all

waters. I was fortunate in being able to fish a lake which, apart from eels and occasional trout, contained only carp. The eels and trout could be a problem. On many waters where fish of other species are prolific the problem becomes magnified. But if you can pinpoint feeding carp then I think you will find floatfished maggots are worth considering.

First night Carp – 1963

Fellow specimen hunter Reg and I started the 1963 season by paying a visit to a small pool in north Yorkshire. The water was a long way from home, which ruled out any question of pre-baiting, and we had to be content with throwing in our bait on arrival – about an hour before dark. The task completed, we rigged up our tackle and carried from the car all the food and impedimenta necessary to sustain us for our two day stay. Then, at precisely midnight on the eve of opening day we cast our first new season bread upon the water, adjusted our bite alarms and sat back to start our all-night vigil.

A long vigil it was too, for although conditions seemed ideal for carping – the water temperature was 64°F and fish were active most of the time – our flake baits remained untouched during the hours of darkness. In fact it wasn't until two hours after dawn that we each had a run that seemed to trigger off a chain of events that nearly drove us crazy with frustration for almost an hour. During those fifty minutes or so we must have had two dozen runs – and failed to connect with any of them. They were mostly fast runs that 'went like trains', but despite striking both early and late we just could not connect with fish that were obviously not mouthing the bait properly. Eventually, however, the spell was broken by Reg who called out that he had hooked a fish, and a good one at that.

For fully ten minutes that carp did almost as it wished; it stubbornly refused to come anywhere near the surface and we were both convinced that it was at least a twenty pounder. Then the fish rolled over suddenly to reveal the reason for its tremendous power. It was foul hooked in the tail thus confirming what I had suspected – that the bait was only lightly held and Reg's strike had neatly removed the hook from the fish's mouth and embedded it in a rib of the caudal fin. The fish was a mirror weighing 13lb. At about 8am I evened up the score by hooking a fish – this time securely in the top lip – and after a firm scrap slipped the net under a mirror of 10lb.

After a 'fry up' of trout (caught in a nearby brook) we decided to have a few hours sleep, but before getting into the sleeping bag I could not resist taking a rod to explore the lake shallows. And what I saw kept me awake for longer than I had intended. At least half-a-dozen carp could be seen cruising about in water scarcely deep enough to cover their backs. The temptation was too much, so I cast out a piece of flake and settled down behind some tall marginal grasses to await events.

During the first few minutes several carp came up to the bait, which I could see quite clearly in the water, gently picked it up and immediately blew it out again. Eventually, however, one fish bolder than the rest sucked in the flake and moved off casually. I struck (startling the life out of a grey squirrel in a nearby tree) and after a brief tussle landed another mirror, this time a nine pounder.

Later that same day I decided to explore a very awkward swim on the opposite side of the lake where Reg, during his earlier perambulations, had spotted three or four fish in the region of 20lb. They were patrolling close to the bank in five feet of water over which stretched the formidable boughs of a sturdy sycamore tree.

Creeping up and placing a bait over the edge was an easy matter, but landing a fish from such a place would obviously be a very different proposition. Still, nothing daunted nothing won, I dropped my bait over the side and flicked in two or three pieces of paste.

When the hoped-for happened and the line lifted and started to move out from the bank, I slapped in the bale arm, struck, and the battle was on. It was fought out on a tight line using only quick-changing rod positions to tire the fish, which was no twenty pounder but a perfectly conditioned, fully scaled carp of 11½lb.

This bonny fighter proved to be the last fish of the trip, excluding two large eels that picked up our lobworm baits during the early hours of the following morning. Not a flying start, perhaps, but one that left us quite satisfied.

Another first night

The evening prior to another opening day found me on the banks of my favourite carp water. The weather – from my point of view – seemed ideal, warm with the sky obscured by thin cloud. There were carp in evidence on the shallows, and after preparing my tackle and bivouac area I passed away the time, sitting behind cover and lobbing out an assortment of bait samples. Breadpaste and crust were totally ignored, as were potatoes, pieces of cheese and sausage-meat. It wasn't until I threw in a few lobworms that the fish showed any interest. The worms were carefully inspected and a couple actually eaten. I reckoned under the 'safety' of darkness they would be mopped up with more confidence.

But now I was faced with a problem, for on this particular water it is usually fatal to put out a worm after dark on account of the number of eels present. I decided to take my chance and at midnight made my first cast using a very lively lob on a size four hook. I was just arranging the line behind the buzzer antennae when I felt it slipping through my fingers at an alarming rate. Trying not to panic, I slapped in the pick-up, struck and at five minutes past midnight netted my first carp of the season, a fully scaled fish of 12½lb. It was consigned to the keepnet and I quickly made my way back to the same swim, feeling more than pleased.

It was hardly likely that I would get another offer for some time due to the disturbance caused by playing the first fish, but I decided to give the pitch another couple of hours before moving into a swim I had baited earlier. Ten minutes after casting, almost unbelievably, the buzzer sounded and I was on my feet playing a second fish which turned out to be a fat 16lb mirror. Two double figure carp by 12.30am! The keeper who lived 400 yards away reckoned that my singing started his dogs barking and awoke both him and his wife!

Two hours later, just as I was wondering why the eels hadn't shown up, I had a third run and tightened into a fish which produced more fireworks than the previous two put together. From the size of the 'boils' it created in 18 inches of water I suspected it wasn't all that big, but my word it was fit! At one point of the scrap it passed me in the 'wrong' direction and I'll swear it ran itself aground on a sloping bank of dried mud.

It was finally netted and turned out to be another fully scaled fish of 10½lb. With the season but two-and-a-half hours old I had three double figure carp in the net. The dogs began to bark a second time. With a pleasant feeling of light-headedness I cast out a fourth lob, expecting at any time to wake up and find it had all been a dream, but, within twenty minutes I was into a fish which knew exactly where it was going from the moment it felt the hook.

The narrow neck of the shallows was flanked on either side by trees whose branches dipped into the water. This fish headed straight down the centre for the deep end of the lake. Such tactics in daylight are not too disconcerting, but if too much line is allowed, especially after dark, the situation can become positively dangerous as the fish has only to 'kite' either to left or right for safety. With this in mind I applied heavy sidestrain hoping to slow the run before it really got under way. But for the first time that night the clutch began to sizzle and when I clamped down hard at the end of a long dash the fish did a sharp left-hand turn and we parted company as it crashed into a festoon of branches.

After tying on a fresh hook I cast out another worm, convinced that anything could happen on such a night. It did. The sky, instead of growing lighter at the approach of dawn, gradually turned darker as the clouds began to thicken. The first few raindrops were large and scattered but quickly developed into a torrential downpour. As a flash of lightning shimmered down the lake I had my fifth run and amid loud crashes of thunder I realised the eels had arrived, at least one had, a small chap of about 1lb. But any eel is one too many when I am carp fishing and I retired to my bivouac.

Shortly after daylight when the storm had eased off I was back at the shallows but there was no sign of any carp. Neither did my baited swim produce any fish, but somehow I didn't care and made my way home feeling quite satisfied with my first outing of the season.

Another first night – 1968

I'm willing to bet that if a poll was taken after 16 June it would reveal a very high percentage of anglers who *missed* the first bite of the season . . . yes, failed to connect with the first dip of the float, first lift of the dough bobbin, first knock on the rod tip. And you know why? Because we lose our touch in the three-month lay-off of the Close Season.

I was just as guilty as anyone. I went carp fishing on the opening night and tackled up two rods ready for the magic midnight hour. At the stroke of twelve out went the first bait. I slipped the line around the antenna of the buzzer and started to bait up the second rod. As I did so the buzzer sounded on the first rod and I jumped out of my skin, positively shaken to see the line simply hurtling through the rings within seconds of the bait being cast.

Well, dammit, carp aren't supposed to co-operate with such alacrity, are they? I hate to admit it but I panicked. Dropping the rod I was baiting I leaped at the first rod, slammed in the bale arm and hit that fish with enough muscle to bring a horse to its knees.

I was smashed, and I deserved it. The clutch was screwed up tight and I had forgotten to release it! But, as I said, it was the bally three months lay-off that did it, not me! Nothing else happened until 7 o'clock the next morning. Heartbreaking, isn't it? – the whole night gone. Then, at 7am, I picked up a 1½lb eel on lobworm! But fifteen minutes later there was a small consolation prize for my stupidity on the previous night when I slipped the net under a welcome 14½lb mirror carp.

For the second weekend of the season I set off on a long promised visit to Jim Eggett's fishery at Hemingford Grey, Hunts., to try for a carp. After a glorious seven days of sun and ideal conditions the weather decided to change and I arrived to find myself faced with rain, gale force winds and a sudden drop in temperature.

Jim had two lakes – the smaller one holding carp to around 20lb. The larger one had fewer fish but some were estimated to run up to 40lb or possibly more – fish which had become notoriously difficult to catch. On my arrival I met Jim Gibbinson – an 'old hand' on the water. Along with a couple of pals he had just spent two fruitless days matching his wits not only against the carp but against almost everything the elements could offer.

The whole water was dotted with tiny islands and had shallows and deeps which alternated every few yards. Consequently, the carp took a lot of finding. But, in spite of the weather, my appetite was whetted when Jim Gibbinson informed me that if I did catch a fish it would almost certainly be not less than 20lb and, who knows, could well break the then existing record!

On the first session I messed around, 'feeling out' the water and hoping the weather would improve. But it didn't, and on the second night, fishing in strong, wind-driven rain, I settled down seriously to try for a carp. At around 1am I was preparing to pack in the whole thing as hopeless, get a few hours sleep and return at dawn, when I had a run. Unable to believe my good fortune I struck and with visions of a forty-plus pounder I spent the next few seconds trying to prevent a lively fish running round one of the islands. I reckoned Jim was having me on – for I eventually netted out a fully scaled carp weighing 9½lb.

Thinking 'something different' might do the trick the next night I baited my second rod with a whole swan mussel, and again my pulses raced when at 2am this bait was taken. It didn't take long to realise I had hooked an eel and had I been specifically eel fishing I would have been pleased to catch it, for it weighed 3½lb.

Jim Gibbinson had also commented that if I only *saw* one of the lake's big carp I would consider my visit to have been well worthwhile. Well I did see one. It left the water like a salmon and the waves created when it dropped back pushed aside the windswept breakers that were coming down the lake. I promised myself I would return when the conditions were more favourable. But I never did.

Crust sipping Carp – 1967

The more I go fishing the more complex, and yet at the same time more fascinating, the problems seem to become. This is never more true than in carp fishing.

About eight years ago a friend and I paid a visit to a 'new' carp water. Within an hour of starting to fish we had both taken a double figure fish each, both on floating crust. This seemed too good to be true so I talked to the owner of the lake, who not only fished it himself but kept a strict watch over the fishing that went on and I got a surprise when he told me that these were the first carp to be taken in this manner.

Thinking we were on to a winner, surface-fished crust played a leading role in the methods we employed on subsequent visits. However, since that first trip we fished the water on many subsequent seasons, but though we caught plenty of carp we never caught another on a crust fished on the surface! What's more, we never saw a fish take any of the loose crusts we liberally scattered over the water on our visits – at least until 1967.

It is frequently the case on a water that is heavily fished that carp will accept a certain bait until such time as they become wary of it, either through being caught on it a few times or because they are hooked and break away. But on the lake in question this didn't apply. The fish just don't (or didn't) accept pieces of floating crust. At least *we* had never taken a fish on this bait since the two caught eight years previously.

That season I sensed a change of heart. On two occasions, while fishing a bait on the bottom, I had casually flicked in a piece of loose crust, unattached, which had been silently taken by a fish right from under my nose – a somewhat frustrating experience! Each time the crust disappeared so silently that I began to suspect that although we hadn't had a crust bait taken in eight years, it was feasible that these 'silent sippers' were surreptitiously taking free offerings without our knowing. In both the instances mentioned had I not been actually looking at the crust at the time I would never have seen it taken.

Before leaving the water on my last trip I littered the surface with pieces of crust broken from two large loaves. It's a thing we had often done in the past but somehow I had the feeling that this time we might achieve some results for our labours.

The following weekend I arrived at the water in the evening and determined to go the whole hog, I put out two rods, both loaded with a crust which was floated just below the rod point. It was a fairly 'light' night and bite alarms were not really necessary. For four hours I watched two pieces of silver paper hanging limply on the line.

At about 2am the paper on the left hand rod rose about three inches. I had heard no sound and neither had I seen any ripple from the water but I sat poised with hands over the rod ready to strike. Nothing further happened and 20 minutes later I pulled in the end tackle to find the crust gone.

As the sky began to lighten I changed bait positions. On one rod I cast a substantial lump of crust well out to my right, and the second chunk to my left, parallel to the bank and close alongside a dead tree which had fallen into the lake. By 7am the sun was on the water and I was beginning to think about bacon and eggs when suddenly a pair of very weary eyes lost their tiredness as the crust on the second rod began to wobble. In less time than it takes to write, the bait had gone and line was sneaking through the rod rings. A few minutes later I had the satisfaction of netting a very plump mirror of 14½lb, the first from the water on crust in eight years.

Breakfast was taken more hurriedly than usual for I wanted to get back on the water before the sun was too high. I fished for a further four hours in the shade provided by a huge oak which overhangs the water. My hooked crust was ignored but two loose pieces which had drifted into the side suddenly disappeared. Finally the craving for sleep drove me to my bed.

It had been an interesting session. Once again the fish I had caught, and the one I hadn't heard or seen during the night, had taken crust with the stealth of an Indian. It is strange how on some waters carp take a crust from the surface with a noise that sounds almost like a pig at a trough, while on others they achieve it with hardly any disturbance at all. It is just one of the complexities of fishing I mentioned at the start. Equally puzzling is the 'fact' (!) that after eight years the fish were again apparently beginning to take a fresh interest in surface baits. Queer fish, carp!

Footnote

These carp didn't really get back onto taking surface baits. The only two fish I fooled was when I put out a crust with a bunch of maggots wriggling underneath on the bend of the hook. This weird-looking bait nailed me a 17lb mirror. The second was an 18lb fully scaled fish. Instead of maggots I stitched some lively red worms to the crumb side of a piece of crust and cast this out on a size 4 hook. I tried it first at home in a glass of water to see the effect. The wriggling worms hung down below looking like some freak jellyfish, what the bait looked like to the fish I have no idea. The worms may look like some oversize larvae hanging in the surface film; but perhaps the fish saw it as a tasty hunk of crust with an attractive bunch of worms attached – and asked no further questions!

Three 'Elite' Carp

Two reels favoured by carp anglers during the fifties and sixties were the ever popular Mitchell 300 and the value-for-money reel, the Elite. This latter came from the Intrepid stable managed by Ken Morrit, who produced a range of British made reels for every fishing situation and to suit every pocket. Literally thousands were sold and I had two which were still in good working order after 25 years of wear and tear. Shortly after they were introduced I was sent one to test and review. I caught a lot of carp while using it as well as specimens of several other species.

The season after the reel arrived I received a call from Arthur Oglesby asking if I could catch him a carp while he filmed me using the Elite. Arthur, whose photographic skills were well known – and still are – had been requested by Ken Morrit to take some film of the Elite in action. As I recall he had provided Arthur with a gift of an 8mm cine camera to do the job. I remember writing to Ken to tell him that on *the day* I would be fishing with two rods, but warned him that on one of them I would be using a Mitchell 300. A second Elite arrived by return of post!

The date and time were arranged with Arthur. I was to turn up at the lake one evening to pre-bait, while Arthur would arrive the next morning, hopefully to film me catching a fish while using the Elite. Fully realising the problems that can sometimes arise when trying to catch a fish for the camera I left home intending to fish all night, working on the theory that, at a pinch, it's better to 'get one in the bag' just in case!

I set off with my old friend, Reg Brotherton, and drove nearly two hours in pouring rain which, by the time we arrived at the lake, had turned torrential. The all-night session was cancelled and we retired to a nearby derelict cottage, which we sometimes used on longer stints, and cooked a meal.

At midnight, with the rain still lashing down, I baited up a swim with four large, stale loaves. These had been prepared prior to leaving by letting them soak overnight, squeezing out the surplus water and then stiffening with bran. Midnight pre-baiting has paid dividends for me not only with carp, but also tench and bream. If a swim is baited at midnight, and a return made at dawn, then fish are frequently to be found feeding in the area. The loose bait, whatever it is, need not be scattered widely but kept in an area twelve foot square. The timing appears to be critical. Should the baiting be earlier then the fish could have eaten up and moved on before you start fishing. The same applies if the return to the swim is made later. I usually get my head down for the four hours of waiting.

The rain had stopped by dawn. I was back at the swim by 4am and put out a piece of flake on each rod. Within seconds the silver paper on the left-hand rod shot up and the line flew thorugh the rings. I picked up the rod, slapped home the bale arm, felt for the fish, struck hard back – and smashed off. I had forgotten to loosen the clutch!

Twenty minutes later I pulled into a heavy fish which, after a short tussle, came unstuck. I was convinced I had blown it. It wasn't an easy water and two offers a session were slightly better than par for the lake.

Arthur duly arrived and I told him the sad story. For nearly an hour we chatted then suddenly the line on the right-hand rod tightened and fell back. The camera was directed to the silver paper which obligingly rose to the butt ring and some good film was shot of an accelerating line leaving the spool. A pretty common carp of 9½lb soon dropped into the net. This was followed half an hour later by a plump mirror of 11½lb. Arthur was delighted. I was amazed at our good fortune, but it wasn't all over. Ten minutes later I pulled into a bigger fish which 'kited' to the right and struggled hard to reach a sunken tree.

I was using a prototype of my new glass carp rod, matched to some 11lb BS Perlyl, and as the fish reached the branches we arrived at a point of now or never. With finger pressed hard down on the spool lip I pulled hard to the left. There came a tremendous flurry of water and a 16lb mirror was, almost literally, turned over onto its back. I remember Arthur saying 'I reckon you have got that rod just about right!' – in fact he was so impressed he had me send him one to use as a salmon spinner.

It was a successful end to a good session. I had caught three nice carp; Arthur had got the shots he required and

Ken Morrit his film of an Intrepid Elite in action. Reg rounded off the film nicely by netting a further carp of 9lb.

Television Carp

In 1963 I did a series of angling films for Yorkshire Television. The task was never easy! Apart from the fact that I was expected to catch fish of a given species in one day's filming (which I managed to do) the job was never helped by the television crew that turned up to make the film. Most of them had never fished and had no conception of what was involved in trying to catch a specimen fish.

To quote an instance of how out of touch they were, my wife received a telephone call one Friday afternoon from the producer of the series who asked 'Can Tag catch us a big carp next Monday!' I rang them back and managed to extend the date for a week in order to give me time to do a bit of pre-baiting.

The team arrived at the lake at 8.30am. I have never known why but there were nine people in the crew – most of whom I think had come along to see me catch a big carp! I explained to all, before we set a foot on to the banks of the lake, what I had planned and also some of the problems of trying to catch carp. There was one tall chap, who stood well over six feet, who enquired how many did I think I would catch? The carp, I told them, on a 'normal' morning, would move down the west side of the lake usually reaching the shallows by 10am or thereabouts. Also that I had baited up a swim there and that with a bit of luck we might get a fish. I suggested that when the cameraman had got himself into position and that when all the recording cables were laid it would be a good idea if everyone kept out of sight as much as possible, and kept quiet.

A huge mirror turned up almost on cue, picking up loose bits of bread paste as it approached. I gave a pre-arranged signal to the cameraman and sat poised with my hand over the rod. At that moment the tall gentleman stepped from behind a tree, at the side of where I was crouched behind cover, pointed out in the direction of the fish and shouted something like 'There's an enormous fish there.' There came one tremendous swirl and the fish departed, never to be seen again.

'Little John' will never know how near he was to being thrown into the lake! We finished the film by dubbing on some canned stuff that I had done earlier, and although this dubbed material had been shot in a different location nobody I talked to noticed the difference!

Carp: The second revolution – 1986

In 1967 I wrote a chapter in David Carl Forbes' book 'Catch a Big Fish' entitled 'The Carp Revolution'. In the first sentence I said: "In this country over the past ten years a revolution has taken place in the outlook of anglers towards carp and carp fishing." I little realised the even bigger changes that would be made over the following fifteen years.

When I wrote the above in the sixties it appeared that a set pattern had developed in tackle, baits and methods that would be with us for centuries. Take rods for instance. The length of a standard carp rod was 10ft, with a test curve of around 1½lb. I wrote: "This, for most kinds of carp fishing is an ideal length and one which is liable to remain with us forever." Today, rods of 11 and 12 feet, with test curves from 1lb to 3½lb are in general use. Also, of course, in many instances, rods are now made of carbon or boron instead of the usual glass fibre. Reels haven't changed much in design and the original, popular Mitchell 300 is still much in demand. A slight modification came along with the introduction of skirted spools and stern drags. There is still a place for a reel with a *longer* spool – not deeper or wider but lengthened so that the spool would not be half empty after a long cast has been made.

Line strength, which on average was around 11lb breaking strain has remained fairly constant although in some cases has been reduced to as low as 6lb. This is due to the fact that much carp fishing is now carried out on large, almost reservoir-like, snag-free waters where even 30lb plus fish can be played and landed.

However, the most startling revolution that has taken place has been in the choice of baits and their presentation. When I wrote the 'Carp Revolution' in 1967, carp baits were virtually the same as they had been for almost 200 years, for example: bread in its various forms, par boiled potatoes, worms and maggots. Occasionally a fish would be caught on some 'alien' bait and I remember the odd carp being caught on flavoured bread paste, pieces of cheese and even marshmallow cubes and bits of banana. Today it would be unthinkable to go fishing without a sample of one of the many varieties of 'boily' baits that are on the market. These high protein, hard skinned baits are responsible for almost one hundred per cent of carp caught each season. Also, because of the rich content of many of these baits, carp feeding on loose offerings are undoubtedly growing at an amazing rate.

But far more of an impact to the carp world, since these fish were first pursued, is the method used in conjunction with the presentation of these deadly 'boilies'. I mean of course the now well known bolt-rig used together with 'boilies' on a hair-rig.

Before the introduction of these deadly rigs carp fishermen went to great lengths to present their baits on a 'weightless' tackle, i.e. nothing on the line except the hook and the bait. We went to extremes to conceal the hook so as not to arouse the suspicions of the fish and when the bait was taken, sometimes after many hours of fishing, the run was frequently missed. Not so today. With the bolt/hair-rig combination carp runs are not only missed less often, but the strain of concentration of waiting of bites has been removed.

Times have also changed dramatically in both the quality and quantities of carp available. In the early sixties a 20lb fish would be given prominence on the front page of the angling press, now it would hardly warrant a mention. Twenty years ago the stocking of still waters with carp was carried out at an ever increasing rate and this has resulted in a prolific number of lakes, ponds and meres, many of which carry a head of mature fish. Thirty pound carp seem to appear almost weekly in angling papers throughout the season.

Finally, 20 years ago, comparatively few anglers would pursue carp after the first frost appeared. It was thought by many leading carp fishermen that carp hibernated, or at least stopped eating in winter and remained in a comatose state until the water temperature rose again in springtime. We now realise that if bait is regularly introduced carp, on many waters, will continue to feed and can be caught throughout the winter months.

Can we go much further? Will there, I wonder, be more dramatic revolutions in the next ten or twenty years?

Conclusion

These days I seldom do any carp fishing. My summers are spent fly fishing for trout and my winters in pursuit of pike, chub and grayling. But I am sometimes asked to give my opinions on the bolt/hair rig, and would I have used them during my carp fishing days.

Reading of anglers driving to the water's edge, putting out three rods and then retiring to the car to listen to the radio, or perhaps have a sleep, to be aroused by the bleep of a buzzer and to find a fish already hooked on one of the rods does make me wince somewhat! When I hear of anglers unzipping and climbing out of sleeping bags, putting on footwear prior to picking up a rod with a fish already well and truly hooked also makes me wonder where the skill and dedication of fishing has gone!

For more weekends than I care to remember I left home on Friday evening to return for lunch on Sunday – sometimes without hardly ever having closed my eyes, and often missing the only run of the session. Let me say here and now that had bolt rigs been available then I would have been happy to have used one. At the same time I must admit there would have been a little feeling of guilt!

Capers after dark

Anyone who has spent any time night fishing will have a few stories to relate, whether funny or otherwise.

There was a period in the fifties when I spent many fruitless hours fishing for carp at Foxon Dam in Derbyshire. This small lake was in a large hollow in the depths of a big wood and was thought to hold no more than half a dozen of twenty pound plus fish which never seemed to breed.

The only man I know to catch one was that fine angler John Neville of nearby Eckington. It weighed 21lb and was caught in 1957 after many days of pre-baiting, together with a lot of patience. One evening I settled down to spend the night at Foxon. There was only one other angler present who packed up shortly after I arrived and after a brief chat made his way home leaving me to the rapidly deepening darkness.

Foxon was a weird place after dark and although night fishing on my own has never held any fears, I know of one or two anglers who felt decidedly uncomfortable while fishing there, and would certainly never dream of fishing at the Dam throughout the night by themselves.

This particular night was really black, one of those sorts to which the eyes never seem to grow accustomed. It was also an unusually quiet night and except for a fox which barked around midnight there was no other sound. From behind me I heard the soft sound of a twig breaking. I turned around and standing immediately behind my chair was the six-foot-two-inch figure of George Barge. I didn't exactly jump out of my seat, but I must admit my heart gave one tremendous leap! George was an excellent woodsman, but so was I, and the fact that he had approached so close without my hearing a sound was somewhat disturbing.

Apparently George, who was a member of the Cormorants Angling Club, was having a drink in his local when the angler I met came in and informed him that I was 'down for the night'. Unable to sleep George, at about 1am, decided to come down for a chat!

There were other less eerie happenings at Foxon. On one occasion, when fishing with Reg Brotherton, I had taken along a deck chair to help make the long hours more comfortable. Due to some heavy rain, which had been falling for two days, the lake margins for about eight feet back from the edge were like a quagmire. We left our seating on dry land and after casting out and arranging buzzers we made our way back through the mire to our respective chairs.

It was a very close, sultry night and around 1am I turned on my side in my deck chair and shortly after must have dozed off. Some time later I awoke to Reg bawling out "Tag, you have got a run." Leaping from the chair I set off in the direction of the screaming buzzer and immediately fell down in the mud. I leapt up straight away and went down again as if pole-axed. The same thing happened again several times and by the time I reached my rods the fish had dropped the bait.

49

The cause of my downfall was that my right leg, resting against the bar of the deck chair had gone completely dead – hence my impersonation of a one-legged man. Reg says it was one of the funniest sights he had ever seen!

The Dam seemed to be a place for 'funny' incidents. Along one side where the margins were perpetually boggy a boardwalk had been erected to enable an angler, or two anglers, to fish in comparative comfort off the end into deeper water.

One night the Thompson brothers, Wilf and Brian, both decided to fish, sitting side by side, off the end. Again the night was very warm and after midnight both fell asleep. At some point in the early hours one of their bite alarms sounded and Brian nudged his brother saying 'Wilf, it's yours.' Wilf, still half asleep, jumped to his feet, turned right and stepped off the boards into three feet of water!

I remember once when Brian pre-baited a swim at Foxon with prawns, hoping to wean the carp into taking a 'new' bait. The following morning, when it became light enough to see, he discovered his swim full of coots that were diving down and surfacing with their beaks full of prawns.

A similar thing happened when I pre-baited with par-boiled potatoes. At first light I had a steady run, which I missed. I looked out over the water to see a coot surfacing with its chalky beak looking even whiter as it tried to engulf my spud!

ROACH and DACE

To do with Roach – 1960

The last outing of the season is always rather sad, yet it is one that I look forward to with interest. Often on this final day the fishing can be good. I cannot say why, but it is so and angling journals reporting on the closing hours frequently confirm this. From all over the country comes news of excellent catches and exceptionally good individual specimens.

My closing trip was spent alone on the river Idle (where I have passed many last days) and I trekked the lengths of the club's fishery to reach a favourite pitch near the upstream boundary fence.

Although I arrived at my swim glowing with warmth from my walk, a biting East wind, which persisted all day, quickly put an end to my feeling of comfort. By the time I had fixed my tackle I realised that this last outing was going to be much colder than many others I had enjoyed.

For the first ten minutes, before starting to fish, I threw in about a dozen maggots about every thirty seconds. This treatment invariably produces a fish on the first swim down, but on this occasion I never had so much as a bite in the first three hours.

At the extreme end of my swim was an area of slack water close in to the bank, so pushing up the float, I allowed the tackle to rest there whilst I fed the spot regularly with maggots. After ten minutes I reeled in to discover that the hook maggots had been reduced to mere skins. The float I was convinced had not registered any sort of bite, so I quickly re-arranged the shotting and made a fresh cast. But no matter where I set the float, or wherever I placed the shots, the maggots still came back sucked 'dry' with no indication being shown on the float.

Filled with curiosity I crept along the bank and, keeping well back from the edge, I watched the float intently as it swung gently in the slack water. In a short time I noticed it move, still without cocking, about an inch to one side. I struck and hooked a fat roach of about a pound. How that fish managed to pick up the maggots without cocking the float I could not say, but I returned to my pitch and started to catch roach, striking whenever I observed the slightest float movement.

The frost had already started to whiten the banks as in the dark I tipped back my day's catch. Alas, it contained nothing startling, no big specimens, but a satisfying net of Idle roach averaging around 14oz with a nice one and a half pounder topping the bill.

If I hadn't caught a fish the day would not have been wasted. In the field across the river a mixed flock of lapwings and golden plover flew into roost, and on the bank opposite was a bed of teasels which were visited on and off throughout the day by a flock of goldfinch. Below me, just past where my float settled, a willow hung in the water and during my stay this was searched by several families of tits including long tailed, blue and great tits as well as a resident robin and wren.

As I was packing my gear a short-eared owl swept across the field and put the plover and lapwing to flight, and overhead, as I walked back to the car, I could hear the calls from a flock of passing redwings making their way to roost. There is a lot more to fishing than catching fish!

Another interesting trip to the Idle was one winter during a freeze-up that almost put paid to any fishing for about three weeks. Still waters were frozen solid and many slow flowing rivers had ice along the margins, and even if you could get through the thick snow to the river banks there were problems of ice freezing in the rod rings.

My best outing was on a brief visit to the Idle, where even areas of this fast flowing river were covered in ice. I made my way along the bank through knee-high snow until I reached a swim on a bend where the current slowed down – although not enough to cause ice to form.

I chose this particular swim for a reason. Apart from the fact that fish are apt to collect in such places, I knew from previous visits under similar conditions that this spot could usually be relied upon to produce a few fish.

There remained the difficult problem of finding somewhere to sit, but once this was overcome I began the task of selecting and rigging suitable tackle. Years of experience of fishing the Idle has proved to me that on this river float fishing is far superior to the leger, under any extremes of weather and water.

On this occasion I chose to use a centre-pin simply because I like to keep my hand in with this now (for me) little used reel. The float I used was a porcupine that I shotted with two BBs – one placed just below the float and the other six inches above a size 16 hook.

Prior to starting to fish I lit a cigarette, and whilst smoking this I kept a continual trickle of maggots going into the swim. I discovered, after a couple of trots down, that my two maggots were tripping the bottom at about four feet. After half a dozen swims the float moved suddenly off course and my strike produced an 8oz dace. In went a few more maggots, and the next trot down brought a roach of similar weight. Amazed at my luck under such conditions I prepared to 'do slaughter', but the following half-hour passed without a bite.

I decided on a change of tactics and by pushing up the float about a foot I allowed the terminal tackle to swing in at the end of the swim and rest alongside the ice that extended a yard out from the bank. This spot I fed with maggots, not heavily but half-a-dozen every half minute or so.

Ten minutes later I withdrew the tackle to find just the skins of the maggots left on the hook. No sign of a bite had I seen, so before making a further cast I loosened the top shot and brought it down the line until it rested against the bottom one. With both shots resting on the bottom the float settled nicely at half-cock, and almost immediately started to tilt upright. Then, just as quickly, it returned to its original position.

After a few minutes I withdrew the tackle to find, once again, two empty maggot skins. Although nearly frozen I decided to make a further adjustment by bringing both shots down to within two inches of the hook. This proved to be the answer, for when the next bite came the float sank out of sight and I netted a magnificently conditioned roach of 1½lb. This was followed by another four ounces less and in the next 90 minutes fourteen more roach between ½lb and 1lb, plus two small chub, found their way into the keepnet.

By this time the sky had darkened considerably. Heavy flakes of snow had started to fall and, not wishing to become snowbound on my homeward journey, I packed my gear and returned to the welcome shelter of my car. The trip back was hazardous but I was quite content. Who wouldn't be with twenty fish weighing approximately 14lb in a little over two hours under such conditions?

Winter still waters

Big fish hunters tend to think of roach in the region of 2lb plus when discussing specimens, but a roach weighing from one pound upwards is a good fish on any water. Still waters that have depths over ten feet, provided they are free from ice, offer a fair chance of catching a hefty specimen and, although you are not likely to take a large bag, you might well land a roach you will long remember, especially on a cold winter day.

Exactly *where* you fish on such waters at this time of year is usually more important than what kind of bait you use. Some fish, like perch, often move into deep water and remain there until spring, but roach, I find, are inclined to move about more and their position in most lakes, reservoirs, etc., is largely governed by the temperature of the water existing at the time. It will be seen, then, that you may have to move your pitch a few times before the fish are located. In summer, when the shoals are more active, they can be fished for in one place and their wanderings arrested by the introduction of groundbait. But during the colder months groundbait needs to be strictly controlled. Your fishing can be ruined by using too much.

We seldom get a winter temperature high enough to start the shoals feeding voraciusly and, generally speaking, a few samples of hookbait introduced occasionally is usually sufficient. Maggots are a good winter bait, but it pays to ring the changes by trying quarter inch cubes of crust, pieces of soft paste or small worms. Baits need to be fished on the bottom most of the time and, although you can use a light leger rig, I prefer a float when possible, which often necessitates the use of a slider when very deep water is being fished.

If a cold spell has persisted for a week or more then it will pay to search the deeper water thoroughly, but after a few days of mild weather the fish could be almost anywhere and you must systematically try both the shallows and deeps. An hour in one spot is quite long enough, and if no bites are forthcoming then move around the banks and try a fresh swim that has a different depth of water.

As you will be fishing waters that are mostly free from snags in the form of weeds you can afford to fish reasonably fine. A line with a breaking strain of 2lb is sufficient for most purposes, unless you are fishing at long range when you can use a line a pound stronger. Hook sizes can range between 18 and 12 depending on the proportions of the bait being used, and type of float is mainly dependent on the weather conditions existing at the time.

You may spend several fruitless visits hunting for big roach, but the time will arrive when you catch fish, perhaps just one, that will make all your persistence worthwhile. I remember fishing a Nottinghamshire lake with the late Jack Smalley, who was the finest roach angler I ever met. We fished a deep spot on the lake and it was nearly dark when I had two bites. The first produced a roach of 2lb 4oz, the second gave me my best roach yet, a wonderfully conditioned fish which tipped the scales at 2lb 12oz.

Most of the stillwater roach fishing available to me consists of shallow lakes and ponds. By shallow I mean depths not exceeding about six feet. And because of that roach fishing in winter can be a waste of time.

I find roach from small running waters easier to catch in winter than in summer. But stillwater roach in shallow waters are a tough challenge once winter has really set its teeth. I reckon that in the depths of winter, the roach in such waters eat very little. In fact I wouldn't be surprised if they remained in a comatose state for weeks on end, if not disturbed by predators.

On this type of water I always have far more confidence when I know there is a good head of pike present. There is no doubt that pike, and to a lesser extent perch, will liven up a shoal of roach that might otherwise lie doggo for days. Once the roach are forced into activity they have to feed to some extent in order to replace spent energy.

In conditions of extremely low water temperatures there is very little difference in thermometer readings at the bottom of ten feet of water and in the shallows. In big reservoirs and deep pits the situation is entirely different for here deeper places can be found where the water is well inside the lower temperature limit at which roach will feed. On both 'predatory' and 'non-predatory' lakes the times to take advantage are during those odd periods in winter when the weather becomes freakish and remains mild for several days. But such days are uncommon and usually most of us have to accept whatever weather the weekend brings.

The natural tendency of the angler during these winter visits is to fish the deeper water. But with an overall uniform set of water temperatures the fish may be anywhere. I've often had better sport fishing the shallows than the deeps. Any sort of surface activity, even the smallest rise, should be taken as a favourable lead and if within casting range the bait should be fished in that area. Half the battle in catching big winter roach, especially on a large shallow water, is trying first to find where they are.

If I had to choose a best time of day to fish then I would choose the last half, and particularly the last hour of daylight. If you can stand the cold then sometimes its worth staying on for an hour after dark, when either the float can be illuminated with a lamp or a light leger rig can be used.

Although maggots will take their share of winter roach I much prefer bread baits for the better quality fish. Redworms are also an excellent bait but small perch can be a nuisance if they are present in any numbers.

The first task when you reach the water is to train yourself not to be in too big a hurry to start fishing. If the surface is calm enough then time spent in searching for fish movement is well worthwhile. Should the surface be too wind-ruffled for observation then I find it best to go in search of the fish instead of remaining in one spot.

Unless moved around by predators a shoal of 'frozen' roach may remain in one place for days on end and no amount of groundbaiting will attract them if they happen to be out of casting range. An hour is plenty long enough to spend without a bite and allows enough time to search a wide arc of the swim. If a fish is caught then I concentrate in that area, often remaining there trying various techniques until I finish fishing.

Most roach will be caught with the bait on the bottom, but if bites are slow in coming after the first fish has been taken then it pays to experiment. This can be a trying task on a bitterly cold day, but it sometimes has its rewards by producing a fish or two that would otherwise not have been caught. For some strange reason the roach may only be prepared to accept a bait fished at midwater, or at any depth between bottom and near surface. At other times they may intercept a slowly falling bait and ignore one that remains static. Trying out different techniques may involve a lot of shot and float changing at a time when both fingers and mind are numb with cold, but they must be tried if bites are not coming.

A cloud groundbait is substantial enough to persuade the fish to start looking for food, and unless roach are feeding in earnest this should be introduced in very small amounts. A heavy groundbait can ruin chances completely.

If a long cast is needed to reach the fish then whenever possible I try to get them on the move by dropping my groundbait a little closer towards the bank. When the light fades it is far easier to pinpoint a feeding area under the rod tip than one which requires a 30 yard cast! If there are any bites at all then they tend to become bolder as darkness approaches. During the brighter hours they can be so delicate that float sensitivity is of the utmost importance.

Roach in small running waters

Small running waters hold far bigger roach than anyone would suspect and sometimes the best opportunity to catch them is during the winter months. It is quite possible of course to take good roach from these places in summer, but I find catching them at the back end of the year is easier.

A knowledge of the water during the warmer months is a great help. You can obtain vital information about depths and the nature of the stream bed a lot easier than you can in winter. With the stream running at normal level, for instance, I believe it essential to know the whereabouts of a clean bottom. Any roach of respectable size will invariably choose such a place in favour of one covered in accumulated silt.

Perhaps I ought to make it clear what I mean by a respectable roach. Some anglers are better situated than others to fish waters holding roach weighing 2lb and over – and I've enjoyed a lot of satisfaction taking a fair share of such specimens myself. But on any water I am always interested in catching a roach weighing more than 1lb. On a small stream I'm delighted. Take it from me, throughout the country as a whole such fish are not caught every day.

I'm not at all sure that there is a best time to catch roach during the day from these waters in winter. Over the years I have failed to discover any definite pattern of feeding and I've had the experience of taking good fish at all hours and in all types of weather. Perhaps I'd give preference to the last hour of daylight, but it's difficult to lay down any hard and fast rule.

I well remember catching roach during a mid-morning snowfall which lasted for about an hour, yet before and after this period when the weather was considerably brighter, I never had another bite. Seldom have I caught fish during prolonged rain, and I count such conditions as the most unproductive – along with the times when ice-floes are drifting down on the surface.

But let's look on the bright side when the stream, cleaned of its rubbish by the autumn floods, is running at normal height and we get one of those days when the air is that shade warmer than usual. At such times I ignore all the slack areas and eddies and search for a run of current that has a bit of 'life' about it. Slow-moving and sluggish places are left for when the river rises or the water temperature is near freezing point.

Tackled up and ready to start, my first task is to spend 15 minutes introducing into the swim samples of whatever I intend using on the hook. Groundbait in bulk is something I seldom use in winter unless I am trying to bring a shoal of fish from well downstream, and even then I use a fairly fine mixture which is widely dispersed by the current.

I love trotting a float whenever I can and unless conditions rule it out I usually start with a porcupine quill of an appropriate size. Although the fish will be almost certain to be feeding on or near the bottom, it's a good idea to make the first couple of trots down with the bait set about mid-water. I have lost count of the number of times when I've taken a good fish on these first exploratory casts. If there are no bites the float can gradually be pushed up the line until finally the bait is gently tripping the bottom.

Next to a clean bottom, I would attach a lot of importance to carrying a good selection of baits in winter. I have a lot of faith in bread – flake, crust, or paste. But it doesn't pay to be dogmatic and worms and maggots can take their toll on the right day.

When the banks are gripped in frost and the stream is carrying a lot of water then I search out the less turbid spots – and these are frequently very shallow areas close in to the banks. At times it it surprising just how shallow a productive swim can be. I've taken some fine winter roach in water not more than a foot deep and I've caught fish so often by dropping a bait close in to the side that I'm convinced they spend a lot more of their time there than is generally realised.

The fish can be caught there by using a little careful thought. Sometimes it is possible to lay-on by casting first into the main flow and then allowing the float to swing round and settle close to the bank. But frequently it is better to use a light leger rig. Bites are usually timid, often indicated only by a lifting of the line from the rod point or by the tilting, but not submerging, of the float.

Whether to remain in one spot or move when sport is slow is difficult to decide. With the water at normal height, and not too cold, I believe it wise to remain in one place. Fish can often be brought into a swim from a long way downstream by controlled groundbaiting. But when the fingers are so numb that it takes twice the usual time to put on a bait, and when the river is hurtling by at top speed, then I seldom stay longer than half an hour in any one spot – unless, of course, I find an obliging fat winter roach.

Roach in fast shallow waters

Many of our rivers have reaches which are both fast and shallow, not above four feet deep and often much less. I was thinking particularly of the river Idle, but there are many rivers which have many miles of this type of water.

Most anglers when float fishing these streamy runs for roach use plenty of shot on the cast in order to get the bait down to the bottom. This is a good method on fast deeper rivers like the Hampshire Avon or the Stour – big float, plenty of weight to overcome the strong undercurrents, etc. On shallower water this heavy tackle is neither necessary nor desirable.

If you are using maggots as bait (which ninety per cent of our roach anglers do use) and they are well scoured, take a handful and throw them out into a stretch of clear water. You will observe that they sink to the bottom after travelling about five feet (assuming the depth is around four feet). The maggots of course will not stay put but will tumble along for yards until they are swept into some side eddy. I have actually followed them along the bank many times and watched them do this. Once in the eddy they will swing round and round, some re-entering the main current and being carried further downstream, but many of them slowly settling down on the bottom.

Now if a maggot thrown in loose will sink, it is obvious that the one on the hook will do the same, providing its progress is not interrupted by the pull of the float.

This shallow water is often clear and the roach in the stretch I fish will not tolerate a string of shot on the cast at any price. My favourite float is a tiny grayling float which requires just one small shot to make it cock.

Sometimes when fishing a stretch of river I have never fished before I throw in a handful of maggots and watch their progress prior to fixing up my tackle. When I have observed where they are settling I then position myself about ten yards upstream of the eddy or backwash.

It is essential that plenty of maggots are taken if one sets out for a whole day. A fairly continual 'stream' must be kept going to keep the fish in the eddy and prevent them following the ones that are washed back into the main current. It is also important to throw the maggots into the nearside of the main current to ensure that as many of them as possible enter the side eddy.

I usually start off using a single maggot on an 18 hook and increase the size of the hook and number of maggots in accordance with the quality of the fish being caught – two maggots on a 16, three to a 14. The float is set a little deeper than the depth of the eddy and the single shot is pinched on about six inches below the float.

In the Idle, as in most shallow waters, there is a fair amount of trailing underwater weed. These weed clumps are soon discovered after a dozen swims down and once they are located it is a simple matter to retard the float a second until the maggot lifts up and over them. When the float reaches a point just past the end of the eddy the tackle is checked. The float will then swing round into the eddy carrying in the bait naturally along with the 'loose' maggots. There should be no wild casting. The tackle can be gently swung out into the current.

If no bite develops after the float has meandered around the eddy for a while, the tackle should be encouraged (by manipulating the rod top) to re-enter the current and move back into the eddy again, along with a fresh lot of loose maggots. Hooked fish should be brought out of the eddy as quickly as possible and played in the main stream where steady pressure will soon tire them.

On occasions, using this method, I have fished water no more than eighteen inches deep and have had some very satisfying catches. So remember, next time you are on a similar water, don't go trying to reach that eddy under the far bank without giving the one on your *own* side a trial – and fish light.

Try some silkweed for Roach and Dace

There are times when it does the ardent specimen hunter good to abandon once in a while his concentrated efforts at catching big fish and to have a go at something entirely different. He can do a bit of 'ordinary' fishing for roach; take part in a match or even dabble with a fly rod. Similarly it would give the regular competition angler a change to leave behind his match tackle and go hunting specimens.

It is with this philosophy in mind that I occasionally spare a couple of hours and go silkweed fishing for roach and dace on Yorkshire rivers. Catching fish on silkweed is almost a forgotten art in this part of the country, and in my home town of Sheffield comparatively few anglers have even heard of it, yet it is a method that will put fish in the net when all others have failed.

Silkweed is the bright green weed that grows on weir-sills and pilings – *not* the green moss that is often found in the same place, but the 'thin' filament-like variety. Most fish eat silkweed, but roach and dace love it and barbel will lay with their faces tight up against the sill wall sucking it off all day during the summer months.

I remember paying a short visit to a weirpool on the River Ure and fished the weed from the sill. There were two other anglers fishing at the same time, using maggots. They had been there all the morning and when I inquired how they were faring they replied the fish were 'off' and that they had caught only one small roach each. When in less than an hour I tipped back 13 dace and two roach they were some-what surprised – not, by any means, at the size of the bag, but at the simple method that had been used to catch them.

If you have never tried silkweed fishing for roach or dace

then here is how to go about it. Match tackle will do fine. A rod of about eleven feet, a centre-pin reel (probably better than a fixed spool for this job) 2 or 3lb b.s. line, a cork bodied float and a size 10 or 12 hook. Shot the float so that about an inch shows above the surface.

Take up a position on the sill of the weir and do your ground-baiting by simply shuffling your feet a few times at the spot you intend to stand. This dislodges particles of weed which are washed down to the fish below – it's as easy as that!

The next task is to bait your hook and this is just as easily carried out by dangling the terminal tackle over the edge of the sill and scraping up a bit of weed on to your hook. This should *hang* on the hook so that it appears to the fish as a natural piece of weed that has been washed from the weir-sill. It can be put on with the fingers but should be teased out (shredded) and not left looking unnatural in a tight ball.

Trot the bait down a fast run so that it just misses the bottom and you will catch your fish. Always be prepared for a good specimen, for big chub are also partial to a bit of 'green silk'.

There is one point I cannot emphasise too strongly, parti-cularly to younger anglers. *Do not* attempt to step on to the weir-sill if too much water is coming down. They can be tricky places at the best of times. And a long handled land-ing net also gives added safety when netting fish.

Drip-feeding Dace – February 1967

I had been indulging in what you might say is a bit of unfair fishing practice. I say this not because the method is illegal or cheating, but because it is not available to every angler except in exceptional circumstances. Let me explain.

For several weekends I had been fishing a swim on a tiny secluded river which contains, among other species, some very good dace, the average weight of which is quite high. I had taken them to 14oz and I got the feeling some far larger specimens could be present. Running into the head of the swim was a narrow, shallow feeder stream which flows fairly fast over clean gravel. The 'unfair' practice I mentioned was to suspend over this stream a tin of maggots which was left to drip and so groundbait the main river swim for several days before my next visit.

It's a tip you have probably read about in books – but I doubt if many anglers ever actually use it. For a start it is not a practice which lends itself to wide rivers or to ticket waters. In fact in these days of overcrowding and vandalism it's not an easy thing to carry out on *any* water except the very remote fisheries. But it can be tried on a suitable small club or syndicate water, provided other members know about your intentions and don't mind.

There are various ways of carrying out a drip-feed programme. You can hang a corpse of either fur or feather and leave it to become fly-blown and eventualuly drip maggots. Such a scheme is difficult in winter though, and in the summer months timing is not all that easy. With suspended flesh you tend to get 'maggot-drop' occurring all at one time. With a punctured tin the rate of drop can be controlled to a great extent by the number of holes in the bottom of the container.

The advantages of such a plan are plain. For several days – while you work and sleep – your swim is fed by a steady trickle of maggots. Not only are the fish brainwashed into searching for and feeding on maggots, but other fish from farther downstream are often brought into your pitch.

You will need to do a bit of homework on your pre-feeder before setting it in position. For one thing you must decide how fast you want the maggots to drip and get a bait tin big enough and sufficient bait. This is easily done at home by punching two or three holes in your tin – just big enough for the maggots to escape one at a time. Suspend this over a larger container and pour in about a quarter-pint of maggots and time how many drop through, say in one hour. It can then be roughly calculated, depending on how long the maggots have to drip, how many will be required and whether the number of holes have to be increased.

There is one little tip to bear in mind. Outside in near freezing conditions maggots are not nearly so active as they are when dripping through the holes in the bottom of a tin in your kitchen. So in cold weather you probably need to increase the number of holes.

Just before my return visit – after putting the tin in place – we had been treated to two days of heavy rain. On the morning I arrived the rain had been replaced by winds blowing at gale force. I was relieved to find my pre-feeder still in position and still dripping merrily away. But the river was in one hell of a mess, coming down thick and brown and carrying all sorts of drifting debris.

With the dirty water flooding down, the fish took a lot of finding. After more than 90 minutes struggling against wind and current I had started to lose hope when suddenly I hooked and landed a ½lb roach. It came from the extreme end of the swim, tight in against the bank. I kept wishing I was on the opposite bank, which would have made float control much easier. From where I was sitting the blustery wind made it difficult to manoeuvre the float into position, and drifting flotsam made legering almost an impossibility.

In the middle of the afternoon, despite the wind having blown my umbrella inside out and despite the water conditions, I began to get a feeling, when I netted the fourth dace of around 12oz, that somehow I was going to catch the fish I wanted.

In the next 15 minutes I popped two more dace of the same weight into the keepnet and shortly after this I hit another fish which at first I thought must be a small chub. I became excited when it finally surfaced ready for netting. It was a *big* dace, well over the pound mark. As the rod bucked with the force of the wind I steadied myself and reached for the net. My hand had closed round the handle when a gust of wind, swirling in from nowhere, hit the inside of the umbrella. The stakes holding the guy ropes were whipped from the soft ground. I instinctively dropped the net and grabbed for the brolly as it took off, and the fish was gone.

When it comes to losing fish, I believe that 'bad luck' plays only a small part. However, on that particular occasion, I might be pardoned for claiming bad luck in the loss of that dace!

Fly fishing for Dace – August 1964

For some time now, during the hot months of the year, I have packed a fly rod in my holdall along with my bottom rods. There are many occasions in summer when fish will ignore conventional baits but will be prepared to accept an artificial fly, fished either wet or dry. Roach, dace, rudd and chub can at times all be caught on fly, and the keen coarse fisherman should not consider himself completely equipped unless he can handle a fly rod.

I paid a brief visit to the River Idle once, arriving about two in the afternoon. The river was extremely low and several anglers were already packing up in disgust, with very little to show. A quick survey decided me to rig up fly tackle, and I made my way downstream to a shallow stretch of the river where the water ran no more than a few inches deep.

On the way I passed another club member who had been there since early morning, trotting a float, and had not yet caught a fish. To cut a long story short, in little more than an hour I had, during the hot part of a very hot day, landed over two dozen fish – mostly dace but with the odd roach thrown in for good measure. Many of the dace were small, but there was the occasional good fish weighing ten to twelve ounces.

They were not specimens – it was neither the place nor time of day for big fish catching – but it was a method of catching some fish when other anglers were sitting without a bite. Adaptability plays an important part in the make-up of any successful angler, whether he be a matchman, specimen hunter or just a 'pleasure' angler. It is possible, of course, to catch bigger fish during the heat of the day, but, as with any other kind of summer coarse fishing, early mornings and late evening usually provide the best fish.

When the banks are not crowded it often pays to roam, but on this occasion I confined myself to one swim because although shallow it had about it a bit of flow which would be providing more oxygen than most other parts of the river.

I use a two piece, eight foot rod which carries a number six line, and it copes quite well with most of the waters I fish. The strength of the leader point is decided upon by the size of fish expected and the nearness of snags.

Generally speaking, coarse fish seldom become pre-occupied with one species of fly as do trout, and it is usually possible to tempt them with one of the following: Greenwell's Glory; Tup's Indispensible; Iron Blue Dun; Black Gnat and Alder.

It is as well to keep on the move on rivers or streams with fly tackle, except perhaps during hot afternoons when the fish may be in shallow well-aerated water, or in the shade provided by weedbeds. The general idea is to cast a fly where the fish are seen dimpling the surface.

The angler wanders along the bank casting a dry fly whenever he spots any sign of activity. Better quality fish seek out some form of shade from hot sun, and such fish can be tried for with a wet fly sunk close in to beds of weed, lilies, etc. The angler must position himself so that he can drop his fly where it will sink and actually drift into (or under) the weeds. Once in place it is slowly retrieved in a figure of eight fashion.

Artificial nymphs can also be used in the same manner, but before being retrieved the fish can sometimes be lured into taking more vigorously by gently raising and lowering the rod point. Bites are indicated by a lifting or straightening of the line hanging below the rod tip and once hooked the fish must be bullied out into the open.

This is mostly a roving sport and the keepnet is best left at home which means the fish are returned as they are caught.

With Jack Smalley at Rainworth Lake

Some of the finest roach fishing I ever enjoyed was when fishing a lake at Rainworth in Nottinghamshire with the late Jack Smalley, who I mentioned at the beginning of the chapter. He was an incredible catcher of big roach from many waters, lived for nothing but roach and steadfastly turned down any of my offers to take him fishing for any other species. Rainworth lake was just a short walk from his house and his catches made there of specimen roach were phenomenal.

When I first met Jack the roach spree, which had remained at peak perfection for a few years, was in decline. Nevertheless, I spent many happy hours there fishing with Jack, sometimes from the bank but more often from a small rowing boat. His knowledge of the water was frighteningly accurate and I would never dream of suggesting where we might fish. It was left entirely to him to choose the swim and although he varied the pitch many times we never failed to catch. We caught many fine roach with several topping that magical 2lb mark.

His best season was in 1962 when between 16 June and the end of September he caught 247 roach between 1½lb and 3lb 4½oz. He took many mind blowing catches but undoubtedly his best must have been when he caught nineteen fish that weighed 46½lb – an average of nearly 2½lb.

There were many such individual catches . . . fourteen roach weighing 27lb 14oz; six fish for 14lb 3oz. On another day he had two roach of 2lb 9oz and 2lb 8oz and a tench over 5lb.

On another visit, as well as four roach totalling 7lb 4oz he added five tench to the keepnet weighing nearly 15lb. One day he particularly remembered when in seventy-five minutes he caught 30lb of roach and tench. In the catch were nine roach, not one under 2lb and two tench scaling nearly 8lb.

I am only sad I didn't get to know him until the water was past its best, but even so I was able to catch my best ever roach from there.

BARBEL – 1960

Barbel are usually – and quite rightly – associated with fast-water swims. But there are occasions when they'll move into stretches placid enough to house a lazy old carp. True, I doubt whether they do this much during the early weeks, except after dark. But as the season progresses, they will inhabit sluggish swims from time to time during daylight hours.

These slack-water swims can be extremely shallow – sometimes not more than 12 inches deep. Often the water is quite clear. Barbel will only stay there in daylight if they are absolutely sure of themselves. I've watched them feeding in such places on our Yorkshire rivers and as you would expect they are very timid – the slightest movement on the bank, or a heavy footfall seeing them quickly disappear to safer quarters.

Even at the start of the season, barbel in the rivers I fish appear to frequent these unlikely swims after dark. I first realised this when once I was making a long cast to fish a fast run two-thirds of the way across the river. In order to achieve maximum sensitivity I had systematically been reducing the size of my leger lead. But I had gone one step too small and the bait was swept round into an area of almost static water below me. As I was about to retrieve the tackle the rod top whipped over and a 4lb barbel almost hooked itself. Thinking this was a fluke, but at the same time curious, I cast into the same spot and took another four fish before daylight.

Next morning I examined the area. The water didn't reach above my knees and the flow there was almost imperceptible.

I still fish currents during the dark hours that have about them a bit of life. But if there is not much doing I never hesitate to try any slack water within reach. As the season advances I believe that many barbel – at least on some of our Northern waters – tend to move more and more into slower waters. Barbel anglers accustomed to fishing fast swims on rivers in the South might find it interesting that we catch fish on the Yorkshire Ouse from swims that require just one swan shot to hold the bait out in mid-river. Only a finely balanced dough bobbin is needed as a bite indicator.

I fished a similar swim on my first all-night session in 1960 and although I only took three barbel – and, as the sky began to lighten, a 1lb perch – there was a period of intense excitement at about 1.30am. My bobbin slid up towards the butt ring and I bent into a fish which tore off line at an alarming rate, running very powerfully and close to the bottom. Several of these strong runs occurred and my pulse began to race a bit when after what must have been 15 minutes I saw the white belly of a fish turn under my rod end. It looked big: so big that I decided I'd use a torch to assist with the landing. I was both amazed and disappointed when I illuminated a 3lb eel. After netting it I found the eel had been foul hooked in the tail!

As far as I can remember I have never before foul hooked an eel. A fairly-hooked eel usually declares itself in a matter of seconds by the curious way it fights. But there was nothing eel-like about the struggles of this fish and I felt a bit deflated after thinking I'd been playing the grandfather of all Yorkshire barbel for a quarter of an hour.

To return to barbel spotted in shallow swims during daytime, such fish are often better approached from downstream and fished for upstream. If it's at all possible to get into position without scaring the life out of them they will usually accept a bait – a big lobworm is as good as any. When feasible it is better to use no weight on the line at all and just hook the worm only once through the 'nose-end'. Let the bait trundle back through the swim, at the same time raising the rod to keep in touch with the worm. The time to strike is when the line stops or begins to fall back faster than the current flow. If you have done any upstream worming for trout then this method works on exactly the same principle.

The usual 10ft Avon-action rod generally used for barbel will do, but if a lot of this style of fishing is contemplated a rod a couple of feet longer is a better proposition.

If I give the wrong impression let me make it clear I'm not suggesting that for the last 50 years we've all been fishing for barbel in the wrong places. These fish are and I suppose always will be residents of fast water and the proverbial streamer weed. What I am saying is that for reasons best known to themselves, barbel will vacate their usual haunts for quieter waters more often than the average angler would perhaps imagine. Given a careful approach they can often be caught there when established barbel swims are failing to produce any results.

Barbel from under the banks – 1961

Barbel fishing doesn't come easy to me. What I mean is that waters containing these fish are too far away for an evening session or even a half day and it usually involves a weekend trip either north to the Yorkshire rivers or south to the Kennet, Hampshire Avon or upper Thames. And as these weekends come around but four or five times in a season I cannot in any way claim to be a barbel expert. However, the accumulated outings made by Reg Brotherton and myself have not been without their highlights, and some of the information we have gathered may be of use to those more favourably situated – from a barbel fishing point of view.

Anyone with any knowledge of these fish is fully aware of their fondness for fast, well aerated water. Every river in the country containing this species has its recognised barbel swims, and it is a certain fact that if you fish them correctly and long enough you will eventually make contact with this superb, fighting fish.

There are times though when no amount of intelligent fishing will produce a fish, and it is generally understood that the barbel are not feeding. In most cases I believe this to be the reason, but some observations, while spending a few days on the Kennet have led me to think that barbel are not always to be found where expected.

At the time of our fishing the Kennet was both low and clear, and had been for some weeks. It was quite a time since anyone had taken a bag of barbel and it had been a case of picking up an occasional fish here and there. And so it was with Reg and I for a couple of days.

But on the third day of our visit a young man, who was working on a nearby River Board project, asked if we would like to see some barbel. To reach them we had to force our way through a riverside thicket and once at the water's edge we had to lean forward and peer under the bank to the right of our position. Here the river had hollowed out a small cavern reaching several feet back under the bank. There was a steady current pushing through this hole and in the bottom of it, lying side by side, were a dozen barbel. Their weights ranged from about 3lb to two fish which looked well into double figures.

The problem then facing us was how to tackle them. A trial approach was made, in thigh waders, from the other side of the river, but branches either side of the hole, plus the swift intervening current, made this a hopeless task. We then decided to clear a way through the scrub to the immediate left of the swim, leaving the branches around the hole intact.

By now the barbel had been frightened away so we began to bait up the swim. Reg returned and fished the spot late the same evening and never had a bite. A light leger tackle was used in conjunction with a number 4 hook; nine pounds breaking strain line (in view of the 'tightness' of the swim) and a Mk IV carp rod. The 'swim' had been heavily baited up with sausage-meat.

The cast made to get the bait into the hole was quite unique – 'casting in reverse' Reg called it. The bait was swung pendulum fashion, and when enough momentum was gained the line was released on the reverse swing, allowing the bait to shoot back under the bank.

The next morning I was in position early and hooked eleven fish, landing seven of them. A good solid pull on the rod was followed in every case by a vigorous tug of war – each fish making a bold effort to remain in its hideout. Once in the open they could be allowed no slack line because of the close obstructions both upstream and down. Two fish I failed to get out and I was well and truly secured to some submerged root. The two larger fish, once they were out in the open, made a bolt downstream and as they were checked at the first snag, the hook tore free.

Twice I have fished the Kennet: once when the river was over its banks, and in this instance when the water was low and clear. On both occasions the normal barbel swims were unproductive. On each visit my fish came from close in or under the banks. There is little doubt that barbel do vacate their swims under such extreme circumstances.

For barbel fishers who have on their rivers heavily bushed, under-cut banks, there may be something here to think about. Since these Kennet trips, whenever I find my usual barbel swims are not producing I have a scrounge around with a pair of polaroids and have, under these adverse river conditions, often saved what might otherwise have been a blank day.

This particular stretch of the Kennet was an ideal fishery. The river was linked to the Kennet and Avon canal by a lake and fishing for different species was available on all three. As well as barbel and chub fishing in the river there were some excellent roach to be caught, after dark, on the canal. The lake held a mixture of fish which included a good head of tench.

We had been invited to fish the area by Fred J. Taylor who called in to visit us on one particularly hot day. He suggested we catch a few roach from the lake to use as dead bait for eels on the river after dark. We sat fishing in three swims that were separated by bushes and after about half an hour I spied the portly Fred creeping past me stark naked with his finger to his lips urging me to keep quiet. He dived over the top of Reg into the lake shouting as he did, in the best Yorkshire he could muster, "Is there any fish in thy swim"!

The sleeping accommodation while we were there is well worth a mention. An old war-time pill box had been cleared out and was provided with beds, table and chairs. The only problem with it was that in the hot weather it became too hot to sleep without leaving the door open and this was an invitation to the local rat population to invade during the night. These were tolerated until one night I was awakened by an extra brave specimen that was sitting on my pillow. After that we put up with the heat and slept with the door tightly shut!

Weir-sill Barbel – 1969

There are literally scores of different methods one can employ when fishing weirpools. The trouble is that weirpools vary so much in their construction that each presents its own special problems, often calling for several different fishing techniques. I have fished around a score of weirpools on a dozen different rivers, and although one or two methods will produce fish on all of them, each requires a separate approach if the best results are to be obtained. To master successfully every species in any single pool would probably take many seasons of regular visits.

I am reasonably familiar with the weir pool at Topcliffe on Swale. Its barbel hold my interest more than any other species, although over the years it has produced many large fish of different sorts. But whichever weirpool I fish I like to try getting a bait under the weir sill. It is not always easy and requires a special technique.

Because of the formidable rush of water pouring over the sill many anglers assume that it requires a heavy lead to hold the bait in position. In fact the contrary applies. What happens when a heavy leger is used is that as soon as the lead strikes bottom and tries to stick there the surge of water coming over the weir hits the line, pulling the lead out of position and swinging it down the pool.

The secret of getting a bait under the sill is to use as little lead as possible. Depending on how far I have to cast I often use a single swan shot link. Immediately the bait hits the water I shake a length of loose line from the spool before closing the bale arm. Most weirs have an undertow and the effect of a light weight plus the surplus line allows the bait to be carried back under the sill where it will settle in comparatively quiet water.

Fishing upstream in this manner one would expect a slack line bite, but in my experience the bite is usually a positive pull down on the rod end as the fish picks up the bait and tries to plunge back further beneath the sill.

During the heat of a summer day fish of many species spend a lot of their time lying under the weir and they are often prepared to feed if you can get a bait to them. You may remember Tom Williams writing about the numbers of good sized fish he saw beneath the sill when he wore his aqua suit and dived into an Avon weirpool.

I once had the pleasure of inviting barbel expert Peter Wheat to spend a weekend with me at Topcliffe. Apart from wanting to catch a Yorkshire barbel Peter was interested to find out for himself whether or not my boast that Swale fish fought harder than his Hampshire Avon barbel was true. We decided to fish throughout the dark hours, usually a good time to try for a Yorkshire barbel. As the night was overcast I suggested Peter tried the tail end of the pool while I settled for a pitch where I could fish under the sill.

Now this Topcliffe pool is full of snags. It is these numerous obstacles which lose the double figure barbel which I'm sure the pool holds. Regular anglers to the water know the drill to adopt. As soon as a fish is hooked it must be held hard and not allowed to get its head down, otherwise even a small fish will become irretrievably snagged. As all barbel fishermen know, it is not easy to keep a big barbel near the surface immediately after hooking and few fish above seven pounds are ever landed here.

I forget how many leads Peter lost during that first night, but he spent most of the time tackling up and in consequence caught only a few small fish which didn't really give him a chance to assess their fighting ability. I did somewhat better with half a dozen barbel, two of them over 4lb with the best a five pounder, which are fair fish for the Swale. Just after dawn I hooked one of the pool's heavyweights, right from under the weir sill, but despite applying as much pressure as my tackle would stand, there suddenly dawned the sickly realisation that the fish was immovably secure on a snag.

On the second night the sky remained open and I suggested to Peter that we would be fortunate to catch any fish after about 1am. This proved to be the case but by 11.30pm Peter, this time fishing halfway down the pool, hooked a somewhat better-than-average Swale barbel. We weighed the fish straight away and I'm not sure who was the most pleased when the balance stopped dead on 7lb.

I asked Peter his opinion about the fight the fish had given and he said that had he been playing it on the Avon he would have expected that barbel to have weighed in the region of 9lb or more.

I managed a couple of two pounders before midnight, but by 2am we decided to get in a few hours sleep. The following day I had to return home while Peter remained for another night. I understand he tried under the sill and caught two average fish and then hooked a grandad of a barbel which finally wrapped him round a snag, leaving him with the problem I have struggled with for years.

Tagging Yorkshire Barbel – 1965

At the beginning of the 1965/66 season the Northern Specimen Hunters Group began a tagging operation of Swale and Ouse barbel. Sadly the experiment came to an end within a couple of years due to the demise of the group but, even in the short term, some startling information came to light which I think surprised most people.

The first interesting fact was that many barbel were great wanderers. I was always aware that barbel moved into certain areas at spawning time and that later in the season specific spots became known, and quite rightly, as 'barbel swims'. I expect other anglers as well as myself supposed, without giving the matter much thought, that these barbel areas held a resident shoal of fish throughout the season and that they might move a few hundred yards or so upstream or down over a certain stretch of river. What I didn't realise, and neither I suspect did many other anglers, is that barbel, at least in the Yorkshire Ouse and Swale, are apparently continually on the move, often travelling many miles, either upstream or down in the space of a few weeks or even days.

The greatest distance achieved by a barbel tagged by a member of the group was fourteen and a half miles. The fastest move was made by a fish which covered twelve miles in thirty-nine days. To me this nomadic tendency of certain barbel has been one of the greatest revelations in my angling life. In some instances a fish had been caught, tagged, weighed and measured and released to be recaught again several miles further upstream and then recaptured for a third time back in its original haunt, all within the space of a few weeks.

Changing rivers, as it were (for example) from the Ouse upstream to the Ure or into the Swale appeared to be a common occurrence. I believe there is a tendency for the Swale, which has shallow, fast runs and deeps, to receive an influx of barbel during early spring with perhaps a falling back to deeper water as the end of the season draws to a close.

Do these barbel movements, I wonder, take place on other rivers, and if so what causes certain individuals to develop these wanderlust tendencies? I mention certain individuals because not *all* barbel in Yorkshire are nomadic. Some tagged fish have remained and have been caught several times from the same swim throughout the season.

As well as Peter Wheat I have had the pleasure of introducing several other anglers to the joys of Yorkshire barbel fishing, and one in particular I especially recall. It was an occasion when I took along a friend who had done practically no other angling except that of fly fishing for trout.

We arrived on the banks of the Swale one evening while there was still enough daylight for me to settle him in a good swim and show him the rudiments of touch legering. By the time it began to get dark he had familiarised himself with the swim and had become quite good at casting a lump of sausage-meat into the right spot.

I settled myself in a pitch about fifty yards downstream and suggested to my friend that he give me a call should he have any problems. By about 2am I had netted a few nice chub and a couple of barbel, when my companion arived to say he had caught no fish and suspected that he was throwing the bait off during casting. I suggested he try a piece of cheese which would stand a better chance of remaining on the hook and he returned to his swim.

About half an hour later I heard one almighty, excited shout, and almost at the same time a fish thrashed on the surface opposite where I was fishing. Quickly reeling in my tackle I made my way as fast as I could along the bank to see what was happening.

To say the least my friend was agog with excitement. He had apparently successfully struck at a pull on the line and was struggling with a fish he was convinced, "must weigh at least eight pounds because its first full-blooded run had taken about fifty yards of line" – obviously the fish which had lashed the surface in my swim!

Not wishing him to lose his first barbel, and not being quite sure how big it *really* was, I offered no advice on playing but when twenty minutes or so had gone by I suggested he put on a bit more pressure and stood by with the landing net.

Finally the fish was brought over the net and I lifted out an average Swale barbel weighing exactly 2½lb! Here was another angler who had been deceived by the fighting power of a Yorkshire barbel.

Conclusion

Over the years I have examined the stomach contents of a few barbel during the summer months and, apart from the odd nymph and caddis all contained good quantities of weed. I believe silk week would make a good alternative bait if only I knew how to fish it! I have to admit that I have not experimented enough. On the few times I have tried it I have been leger fishing. On two occasions I received a terrific thump on the rod top, but failed to connect. Fishing a piece of silk weed under a float might be the answer.

Another bait which I thought would bring a response from barbel is a slug. I would name it as my number one bait for chub fishing, so why don't barbel accept it with the same gusto? I have fished slugs in swims where both species were present, yet the only reaction came from the chub. The bait was apparently refused by the barbel. I have caught only one barbel on slug: it was a Swale fish and weighed over 7lb.

The most powerful memory I have of barbel is of a fish I hooked in the Swale weirpool at Topcliffe one morning at 4.30am. Reg Brotherton and I had decided to fish the bank opposite to where we normally sat. Not many barbel were caught from there, but there was a run of fast water about three feet deep that ran close in to the bank and we wondered whether, if undisturbed, it might hold a fish or two.

I settled in a pitch about 25 yards above Reg who had decided to tackle the pool tail from a different angle. I was legering a lump of sausage-meat about four feet out from the bank and I hadn't been fishing long when I connected with a fish that had given a good pull on the rod tip. I was using a carp rod matched up with an 8lb line and I was determined the fish was in no way going to cross the river into the treacherous snags which littered the far side. The rod bent alarmingly as I applied heavy sidestrain, but each time the fish was turned and it regained an even keel, it would set off again – desperate to reach its sanctuary.

Finally I suspected it was beginning to tire and although I hadn't seen it I realised it was big. I could not recall ever playing anything with so much power. I shouted to Reg to help with the netting when suddenly it turned quickly in to the side and made a long dash down the fast water close in to the bank. I clamped down hard and 25 yards down-stream, where Reg had just risen to his feet, the fish floundered on top. It looked enormous from where I stood and Reg stood on the bank open-mouthed, only a couple of feet from where the fish was rolling. I had it beat, it was knackered and it was just a matter of netting it when suddenly everything went slack.

Reg wandered slowly up towards me (he told me afterwards I had turned a funny colour!) as I examined a number 2 hook that had been straightened. After a while I enquired "What do you reckon it weighed?" "I have no idea," he replied, "but I can tell you that fish was all of three feet long!"

BREAM

Legering – 1954

Until the 1950s, comparatively few anglers seriously regarded leger fishing as more than a chuck-and-chance-it method of taking fish. By 1954, I was noticing on my fishing outings that more and more anglers were discarding the float in favour of a dough bobbin or some other type of bite indicator, especially since the big fish vogue developed. Even so, with this increase of leger enthusiasts, the chuck-and-chance-it style of fishing still existed.

Methods of legering are almost as legion as in float fishing and the tactics used can decide the difference between a good or an indifferent bag at the end of the day. I was always experimenting and trying to improve my leger fishing, and although it is difficult to set down any hard and fast rules in angling I discovered one or two things which may have helped other leger men towards better catches.

First let me say this. Unless the water being fished is very fast running or an exceptionally long cast is necessary, it is far better to do without any leger weight on the line whatsoever unless it be one shot nipped on about four feet from the hook. This ensures that the terminal tackle is lying straight and flat on the bottom.

Legering is usually practised with the intention of catching good size fish and in most cases the large bait used is sufficient weight in itself to make a fairly long cast. If a leger is used then the Arlesey bomb is the answer, being so designed that whichever way a fish runs with the bait, weight resistance is cut down to a minimum. The only fault in using an unweighted line, especially if fishing under the far bank, is the failure of a fish to register a bite when it picks up the bait and runs in towards the angler. Even electric bite alarms fail to solve this problem completely.

At that time, comparatively few anglers possessed these bite alarms, with most of us still relying on dough bobbins, silver paper or a 'nod' of the rod end etc. These methods if correctly used can still be extremely successful, especially in daylight hours.

Turning now to fish running in with the bait. I once enjoyed a satisfying outing legering for bream. I had returned one and a half stone of these fish to the water all between 1¾ and 3lb in weight and half of them were fish which had picked up the paste I was using and run in towards my side of the drain. After making a cast and tightening up, a piece of paste was pinched on to the line, of which about 12in was drawn off the spool between the first and second rings. The pick-up was closed and the bobbin hung a foot below the rod which I supported with two rests. With a normal bite the bobbin moves up towards the rod and the strike is made immediately the line tightens up. In nine cases out of ten, if the quarry is bream, a strike thus timed will usually connect.

In the second instance – a running in bite – the indicator acts differently. There is usually a slight lifting of the bobbin as the fish picks up the bait and then, as the fish moves in towards the angler, the bobbin returns to its normal position and then drops further back still towards the rear rod rest. The following action is successful seven times out of ten. Pick up the rod, make four or five quick turns on the reel handle and strike.

When legering for bream and the fish appear timid – i.e., the bobbin rising a few inches and dropping back to normal – I often find that by reducing the hook size down to a number 12 and the paste to the size of a pea the bites become more decisive. A number 12 eyed hook tied direct to the line has an amazingly strong holding power, although of course, one feels safer with a larger size – especially on a weedy water where the fish run to a good size.

A strong wind can be just as great a nuisance when legering as when float fishing. A sudden gust catches the line and the bobbin dances up and down making bites difficult to discern. Two things can be done here to eliminate this trouble: (a) lower the front rod rest until the end ring is almost in the water leaving less line exposed between rod tip and surface, or (b) rest the bobbin on the ground, preferably on a ground sheet. The only fault with (b) is that the bobbin will not register 'running in' bites, although should it lift and then drop back to the ground, the method already mentioned will often take fish.

The groundbait for still or semi-still waters should not be the usual mixture of bread and bran – it is far too 'feeding' –

1. The "Barnes Trophy" team, all surnamed Barnes. Left to right – Frank, Alf, Albert, George, Tag and my father, Ernest.

2. (right) Trying to catch a big chub for Yorkshire Television.

3. A double figure carp weighed in a rabbit net. This picture, which appeared in the angling press, began a long correspondence between the author and Fred Taylor – another rabbiting man.

4. Four double carp in one night and a thirteen pounder of Reg Brotherton's.

5. A big carp – safely netted.

6. Suspended maggots drip a dace – swim in the main river. This was left in place for two days before starting to fish.

7. A catch of unexpected big rudd taken on a carp exploratory trip.

8. Big roach weighing up to 2 lb 4 oz from Rainworth Lake, fishing with Jack Smalley.

9. Yorkshire Ouse barbel being measured and tagged by members of the Northern Specimen Hunters Group.

10. A five-hour catch of tench averaging 3 lbs from Drax pond.

11. Two "uncatchable" Great Ouse bream.

12. My best ever chub, 21 inch and just six pounds, taken from the Great Ouse.

13. Tag returns another good day's catch at Horhsea Mere.

14. A twenty-plus pike taken by the author from a fifteen foot wide drain gets the dental treatment.

oundbaiting with my "spratapult" at Hornsea Mere.

16. My best ever "unwanted" eel weighing 4 lb 4 oz, caught on cheese after dark while legering for chub.

17. A brace of three pound perch from the Derbyshire Derwent.

18. A 2 lb 2 oz grayling from the Driffield canal.

19. My best ever brown trout of 9½ lbs from Ladybower reservoir.

and I find the best results are obtained by using a liberal amount of sausage rusk or a fine powdered cloud bait, well wetted and sqeezed tight.

Legering for bream in fast water calls for different tactics. The leger weight should be an Arlesey bomb large enough to hold the hook bait among the groundbait. The rod should be held in the hand with the reel pick-up closed. The response to a bite which will be observed by a 'nod' of the rod tip should be immediate, but *not* violent. I mention this because our natural reaction to a savage tug on the rod is to strike with an equal, and often fatal, ferocity.

Groundbait for fast waters is the stuff usually recommended for bream – bread and bran and plenty of it. If the current is exceptionally strong, a stone or pebble added to the centre of each ball will help it to arrive at the bottom in the right place. A visit the following week to this narrow Lincolnshire drain produced a further net of bream among which was my best to date weighing 6lb 12oz.

One of the most interesting bream problems was posed by a small shoal of fair sized fish on the upper reaches of the Great Ouse. I had been invited by Dick Walker to spend a week there, and his fishing hut was placed at my disposal. I was really supposed to be chub fishing when I spotted them – a shoal of about a dozen fish basking in a clear patch amongst lilies and bulrushes. I guessed their weights would range from 2lb up to possibly 7lb.

These bream intrigued me because they had a hard-to-catch reputation. Although they had been observed in the same area on and off throughout the summer months for several years, as far as I could ascertain not one of them had been caught. That was why I decided to spare them a little of my chub fishing time.

I started by applying a principle I had used successfully when fishing for bream previously on small running waters – a liberal baiting up with bread groundbait at midnight. And then, the following morning at first light I was back at the swim tackled up with a 7lb line and a number 8 eyed hook. The bait was a big lump of soft paste used without either float or lead.

The first hour produced no bites so I scaled down the line to 4lb, the hook to a number 10 and the paste to the size of a pea. Almost immediately after casting out the line hanging from the rod end lifted and then fell back. This happened on the following four or five casts, and I decided I would strike at the next movement of line. The outcome was a bream of 4lb. Twenty minutes later the line lifted again and after a short tussle I slipped the net under a fine specimen, two ounces short of six pounds.

The following morning found me 'chasing' chub, and this time the bream swim was baited-up at 6pm in preparation for an evening session. I had no bites before dark so I held the line in my fingers, hoping that if any bites did come they would be bolder than the ones in daylight. There were three pulls altogether. The first two were gentle ones from bream, both of which were hooked and came off in quick time. The third bite was a vigorous affair which almost certainly came from a monstrous chub that I had seen cruising round the swim early on the first morning. There was a tremendous pull on the rod as the fish bore off towards the bulrushes, and as I applied sidestrain the hook tore out and the rushes shook violently as the huge fish ploughed its way through.

The rest of my stay was occupied hunting chub, but those bream presented a problem on which I would dearly have loved to have spent more time. Despite their general lack of 'staying power' when hooked, the initial dash of a large bream in a *tight* swim can easily pull out a small hook when pressure is applied; yet when I used a bigger bait on more substantial tackle I didn't get the bites. Would the regular introduction of larger samples (instead of groundbait) over a period of time eventually bring them round to accepting a bigger bait?

During the remainder of my stay I half-heartedly tried out several experiments on those bream during the heat of the day when they were basking in the sunlight. I presented them with various artificial flies and nymphs and I tried them with tiny dead minnows, rigged so that they wobbled slowly past their noses. All to no avail.

My half-heartedness was probably the main reason. Catching any specimen of any species, including bream, demands one's undivided attention. While I was messing about with the bream my mind was on the Great Ouse's splendid chub. Still, I had the satisfaction of landing at least one 'uncatchable' fish of a respectable size.

CHUB

It has often been suggested that there might possibly be an easily measured intensity of light at which certain species of fish will feed at their most determined. The theory is supported by the fact that the majority of fish feed more enthusiastically in the half-light of dusk and dawn, although I would hesitate to attribute this to some magic reading on a light meter.

The reason, I believe, is simple and is nothing more mystical than the fact that, like most hunted creatures, a fish feels safer and more secure in a subdued light. Having written that I expect someone will suggest that this theory doesn't apply in winter and that fish often feed only for a short spell around mid-day; which of course is often the case. But experience over many years has satisfied me that even in the coldest winter some fish will only start to feed, often with gusto, as darkness begins to close in.

Particularly have I found this so with chub, although I have known roach, grayling, perch and pike to be similarly affected. It may sound strange that the last two mentioned species (which hunt chiefly by sight) should be included, but it is a fact. On a number of occasions I have, early on a winter's morning, taken both these fish as soon as it has become light enough to cast. At Hornsea Mere pike are frequently landed during the last few minutes of daylight but chub, especially, will often wait until 'owl-light' before commencing to feed. Then, for a short spell, I have known them 'go mad', often feeding without any apparent caution whatever.

There was one occasion when I fished the river Wye with a group of fellow specimen hunters. We spent all day pursuing chub by orthodox methods with little success. Then, as it began to get dark, one of our party began catching chub and in twenty minutes he had six good fish on the bank, all taken from the spot where he had spent the day legering without a bite. The remarkable thing about all this was that while five of us (who had packed up fishing) pranced up and down the banks making a hell of a row and taking photographs with flash, our friend continued to catch chub. Those fish just would not be upset by any amount of noise and disturbance.

I have known such odd behaviour happen on a number of different rivers, and I have had similar experiences on the rivers Bain, Nidd and most of the Yorkshire rivers. I once fished the upper reaches of the Nidd with the late Tim (TK) Wilson with hardly anything to show until the last hour of a cold winter's day when we both began catching a chub at every cast.

Once on the river Bain in Lincolnshire, after sitting bite-less all day by a pool that I knew held some good chub, I landed five fish between 2½ and 5lb in the last thirty minutes.

The two best chub I ever landed from the Idle came to the net as darkness was falling – after fishing for six hours without a bite. I recall once spending all day fishing an ice fringed river Wharf when the chub did not commence to feed until it was almost too dark to see the rod tip, and then went on to take three fish between 3½ to 5½lb.

Such instances have given me food for thought inasmuch as I wonder whether I might catch just as many fish by arriving at the water after lunch, instead of sitting out a full seven or eight hours in the cold!

I remember fishing the Swale on a winter's day of low water and bright sunshine. Bites were few and far between and a stroll along the bank revealed a lack of fish being caught anywhere. Line strength and hook size were dropped down far beyond the 'safety limit' in an effort to deceive the bigger chub, but to no avail, so I decided to stay on for an hour after dark to see what could be achieved.

The result was three chub on the bank weighing 1½, 4½ and 5lb, plus two unexpected barbel which were hooked and lost. Chub will often move into the shallows, even in winter, in the late evening and if conditions are right they will remain there until early morning. It is almost certain that these nocturnal feeders are searching for bullheads, leeches, crayfish, etc. (that emerge at night from their day-time hiding places beneath stones and weeds) and they make excellent baits for big chub.

Even stranger behaviour occurred once when fishing the upper Witham with Reg Brotherton on a river that was in an appalling state – flooded, ice cold, and with a piercing wind.

Just prior to calling it a day, without having seen a fish, Reg noticed a trail of breadcrust coming downstream, dumped in no doubt by some retiring angler higher up. As these crusts passed under a willow bush – where Reg's bait was lying – several chub rose to intercept them.

Now no one expects chub to rise to a floating bait under such adverse conditions at the end of a winter's day. But, recovering from his surprise, Reg changed his tackle, floated down a piece of crust and caught chub!

Chub, willows and current speeds – 1961

Ask any angler with which tree he associates chub and he will invariably reply "the willow" and, of course, he would be quite right. It has been appreciated for centuries that the place to look for a chub is beneath a bankside willow tree – or sally bush. You could also ask the same angler *why* one expects to find chub beneath a willow and the inevitable reply is, "Because of the food in the form of insects that drop from the tree." A more knowledgeable angler might follow this up by telling you of the fondness of the fish for the 'withy-bobs', the Bufftip moth caterpillars, that live in these trees.

It is quite true that chub have a taste for these juicy creatures, but I feel just as certain that they are not the reason for the fish's presence beneath the willow. In fact I very much doubt whether willows or any other variety of waterside tree attract chub primarily because of their food holding content. If this were the case then surely, on a mixed fishery, these well-known chub swims would hold a wealth of other fish species, all ready to take advantage of the 'offering from above'! Let us examine the case a little closer.

On some waters where there are an equal number of, say, alders and willows, it is possible to expect just as many chub under the former trees as the latter. On rivers where willows do not exist, but trees overhang the water, be they oak, ash, beech or others, one can hope to find chub beneath them.

And what do we find on a chub-holding river where trees are few and far between? Where do we look for our fish on these un-chubby stretches? In summer they are usually found sheltering beneath luxuriant weed or rush beds. In winter we can search for them lurking below a high bank; underneath a platform of rubbish which, on its downstream journey, has accumulated against some obstruction. Or, if bridges are present on the fishery, around the bridge buttress. In fact chub can be expected anywhere where there is some sort of cover – *provided the current is satisfactory.*

Willows are undoubtedly favoured because often their *spread* is both wider and nearer to the water than other trees, giving a greater feeling of security to the fish beneath. But the retreat below an old, permanently tethered barge would do just as well – *providing the flow of the current is satisfactory.*

Chub, probably more than any other fish, insist on the nearness of some form of overhead cover and should this be lacking then the next best thing is chosen in the shape of high banks, bridges, etc. – *so long as the pace of the current suits the fish.*

Many of us are familiar with a tree-lined stretch of river which, despite the similarity of the trees – from a food producing point of view – give up chub in any numbers only in certain swims, while others provide only the occasional fish.

The novice chub angler will have to decide from experience what constitutes a 'suitable current'. He will be on the right track if he searches for a swim that carries a fairly good flow. At any time of the season chub seem to prefer a good 'flush of water', and if this can be matched with some form of cover the angler is part way to success.

Even good swims cannot be guaranteed to hold fish *all* the time. I have in my mind one particular chub-holding swim beneath a willow which most of the year carried just the right volume of water. Thirty yards upstream stood an almost identical tree under which the water ran much slower and which, under normal conditions rarely produced a fish, except during periods of flood. At these times the first swim obviously became too fast and untenable for the chub, so they moved upstream to the second tree where the increased current was now more to their liking.

A 'withy-bob', good bait that it is, is not a bit of good fished in the *wrong* swim. But find the *right flow* under any sort of cover and you can fish with almost any old bait with confidence.

Strange Chub Behaviour – 1960

I was always under the impression that chub, large chub, never moved far from a favourite haunt in a river. Extra big chub usually find themselves an individual hole and rarely stray far from it through the season. Normally a school of two or three fairly large fish will stick rigidly to one beat, patrolling up and down at reasonably regular intervals.

After one particular chub outing I started wondering just how much we really could accept as fact in matters piscatorial!

I reached the upper Witham late on the Friday evening of an August weekend and, after a quick fish-spotting reconnaissance, bedded down for the night in my sleeping bag. The following morning at first light I set off doing 'Indian crawls', casting a lobworm into places where good chub had been sighted the previous evening, feeling confident I should get at least one sizeable fish.

I had slowly worked my way upstream with nothing to show except a few minor chub. The water seemed devoid of specimens and by the time I had reached the last fence before a bridge I was feeling somewhat perplexed. My approach I felt certain wasn't at fault and I knew these particular chub had a passion for lobworms.

As I arrived at the last fence I heard a commotion in the shallows immediately below the bridge. The splashing was so loud that I heard it first from a distance of fifty yards before I saw it. The water was being churned up into such a turmoil that I thought it must be an otter struggling with an extra large fish.

Carefully I approached and as I peeped over the rushes I observed a sight which set my pulses racing. Hurtling themselves against the rapid bubbling water in a frantic effort to cross the shallows was a shoal of some thirty chub. I doubt if any were under two pounds in weight; many were nearer to six. They reminded me of running salmon in their urgency to get upstream. Would they, I wondered, in their wild thrashing struggle, accept a worm? It took me but twenty seconds to get into position, crouching low near the piling of the bridge facing this advancing, formidable 'armada'.

The first lob I sent rippling down over the stones was taken with such violence that I instinctively reacted with a similar ferocity and clattered the rod against the stonework of the bridge – that one I missed! The second worm was snatched in the same manner and a somewhat calmer strike connected with a heavy fish which came unstuck almost at once. The third lob dropped into the centre of the 'boiling' mass and in less than thirty seconds I had hustled a four pounder into the net.

Normally I would have returned this fish to the water after weighing, but with visions of photographing an extra-ordinary catch of chub I decided to fetch my keepnet which I had left three hundred yards away. After securing the fish in my landing net and submerging it in the water I hared down the bank. In five minutes I arrived back breathless, transferred my chub to more spacious captivity and returned to the 'slaughter'.

There was no sign of a fish. The river had reverted to its normal self, gently flowing over the stones. For some time I watched hoping to see the shallows once more erupt, but in vain. Where, I pondered, had they all gone? Four hours of concentrated fishing of this bridge hole failed to produce a single chub, only unwanted perch shredded my lobworms.

A search of the river both upstream and down failed to locate the shoal. Why this 'migration' of large chub? And how long had it been in progress – since dawn, all night? If only I had started my chub chasing at the bridge instead of wasting a couple of hours crawling around the under-growth!

These fish were certainly not late spawners for as soon as they reached the quieter water beneath the bridge they shot off upstream at top speed. And another thing, I have never known any fish that was actually spawning accept a bait so avidly.

I have never witnessed anything like it since, and many of the country's top chub anglers to whom I have spoken have never seen such behaviour. It is one of those strange phenomena we shall probably never solve.

Upstream legering – 1962

Upstream legering was, at that time, undoubtedly practised more by specimen hunters rather than by other anglers, but even amongst the big fish boys it was still a much neglected method. The reason, I suppose, was because legering a bait upstream was alien and contrary to all we had previously learnt about coarse fishing. The line hanging from the rod tip that indicates a bite by suddenly dropping slack instead of tightening requires a certain amount of readjustment on the part of the angler. And if we are accustomed to ground-baiting a downstream swim, letting the current carry the bait, we are apt to feel somewhat lost when faced with the task of baiting a swim above where we are fishing.

In most cases upstream legering is carried out during the summer months when we can cast our bait to a fish we can see or into a known fish-holding swim. At these times groundbait is seldom necessary. Where I believe we slip up, however, is in neglecting to use the method during the colder months of the year.

Friend Reg and I paid a visit to the river Bain to have another go at its chub, this time accompanied by club member Frank Whiteley. It was Frank's first visit and we placed him in a swim that invariably produces a fish, although we didn't hold out much hope on this occasion because of seven degrees of frost present. However, by the end of the day he had managed to net six good chub, all taken on lobworm legered upstream.

In the meantime Reg had spent much of his time wandering and casting a line into various likely spots. It was interesting to note that the fish he caught all came from one swim – under the branches of a willow that on this particular day was carrying just *the right push of current below it*.

Whilst they were going their various ways I had pushed on well upstream to a bridge beneath which, on our last summer visit, we had seen a shoal of chub. This time the river was coloured and the fish were not visible, but nevertheless I decided to fish the swim and started proceedings by throwing a handful of worms into the water at the other side of the bridge.

In this particular swim one had no option other than to leger upstream, for the fast water above the bridge is culverted between high concrete walls. But despite the pull of the current I found that the bait would hold in position with only one swan shot pinched on the line. I soon discovered too that the cast needed to get the bait well under the arch required correct timing and accuracy; if the bait was not thrown far enough no bites were forthcoming. Even when the bait did reach the right spot the bites were not exactly plentiful. During the first two hours the line from the rod point only fell completely slack on five occasions as a fish picked up the bait and moved towards me. Four of my strikes connected and each time I hit a chub of between 2lb and 3lb. But the big grandfathers of the shoal I had observed during the summer months continued to elude me.

The third hour was a complete blank, so I decided to bait the swim with cheese. Half a pound of it went in above the bridge, but before I could test the worth of this fresh bait a party of schoolchildren escorted by their teacher came along the bank. As all children will, and as I feared, they made straight for the bridge and amused themselves for ten minutes jumping up and down on the planks and dropping stones in the water.

There was nothing to do but wait until these healthy youngsters moved on, but not surprisingly, with all the disturbance, I caught only one more fish, again on an upstream legered lob.

Reflection since then has convinced me that even in winter upstream legering has several advantages over other methods, not least the fact that you are *behind* your fish and there is less chance of them seeing you. It also seems less disturbing to a shoal when one of its members is quietly pulled downstream instead of thrashing and struggling against the current.

The secret of success with this method lies in using a weight that will only just hold bottom. This ensures that when a fish picks up the bait and turns downstream, as it usually does, it feels only a minimum of resistance. It is surprising how little lead is required in even the strongest of currents.

Leger laziness

On a further trip to the Bain we again took along Frank who chose to settle in the swim from where he extracted six chub between 2lb and 3lb on small pieces of crust legered upstream. Reg pushed on upstream to try his hand under a willow, while I went downstream to try a 'new' spot below a small weir. I had in fact fished it before – for the last hour – on a previous visit, and in those 60 minutes I had netted two three pounders and one of 2½lb.

This time I intended spending the whole day in this one swim and had taken along a quantity of groundbait. During the first three hours I alternated huge chunks of crust and cheese on a size 4 hook, and never had a bite. Then, knowing that chub will sometimes refuse big baits in conditions of low water temperatures, I changed the hook to a size 10 and reduced the lumps of crust to quarter inch cubes. The bites came straight away but they were delicate, finicky knocks that would have tested the patience of any angler. I had begun to suspect small dace or roach until I hooked two heavier fish that came unstuck straight away.

It was then that I tried a method that is seldom used by specimen hunters when chub fishing. Removing the leger lead I rigged up a long bodied float which was set two feet deeper than the swim. The lead was replaced by a shot of sufficient size to sink the crust and hold it on the bottom. Barely had the float settled in position, lying nicely at half cock, when it tilted and disappeared. My strike produced a chub of 2½lb and this was quickly followed by another of similar size.

Then came a lull for half an hour before the float sailed away again and this time the rod plunged and bucked to a thick-shouldered fish that took the balance down to just beyond the 4lb mark. Nothing further happened until late in the afternoon when I netted two fish in fifteen minutes, one of them a few ounces over 3lb and the other a couple of ounces short.

I have thought a lot about those five chub since and also how we specimen hunters are apt to become 'leger conscious'. The smaller baits obviously solved the bait size problem on this occasion but, I wonder, would I have caught those fish if I had stuck to legering? I doubt it! Those timid bites on the rod tip were registered with far more definition by simple laying on with a float. I resolved that in the future, whenever chub were biting shy, and if the swim lent itself to the use of a float, I should not hesitate to remove the leger lead. Chub swims of course are not always suitable places in which to employ a float, but many of them, especially in winter, can be sensibly tackled without scaring the fish.

Chub from under the bank

I was disappointed on one chub outing to the Yorkshire Ouse to discover much of it was barred to anglers due to Foot and Mouth disease restrictions. It was a Sunday morning and the quiet country lanes were busy with 'angling cars' all searching for water free from bans. Finally I found a length which for some peculiar reason had been re-opened, and joined a dozen or so anglers already present.

By lunch the situation had become untenable – at least as far as any self-respecting specimen hunter was concerned. The crowds on the banks had been swelled by other anglers until the whole place resembled a popular brewery match. The high flood banks didn't help either, for the 'wanderers' among us insisted on walking along the top instead of at the bottom of the slope at the other side. I collected my gear and began a long walk downstream, determined to find somewhere quieter, or try a different venue.

The last angler was sitting 100 yards before the boundary fence. At least, I decided, if I settled myself by the fence I wouldn't have anyone below me. Furthermore, it was one of the most attractive swims I had seen on the fishery. A small beck entered the river smack by the side of where I sat and it didn't take long to detect the influence its flow had on the main river.

The first thing I did was to send down a few pieces of crust on the surface and study their route after they entered the parent stream. Initially, they moved out several yards into the river and then under the force of the current swirled in close to the bank into an area of steadier water about 30 yards downstream.

Next, I ran down float tackle and discovered that from the fence downstream was a shallow reach which, I surmised, would be a natural collecting place for any food washed out from the beck. I now realise it could be a dumping ground for all kinds of debris and silt and we all know that, where possible, chub prefer to feed over a clean bottom. Light legering on this bank was disappointing, producing only half a dozen small chub by mid afternoon, so I decided to take some action. The Ouse was remarkably clear for the time of year and this, combined with a bright winter sun could well be the culprit.

I entered the beck about ten yards upstream from its mouth and with my feet and a hefty stick proceeded to give the bottom a good old stir. When I returned to my swim a very satisfactory patch of coloured water was seeping out and clouding the river, following exactly the same trail my crust had taken. Within seconds of my casting a lob about 15 yards downstream, the rod end twitched and a chub just under 3lb came to the net. This, I thought, was the answer and with growing confidence prepared to do battle. But nearly an hour later my 'tempting cloud' had disappeared and I hadn't had so much as another bite.

Repeated 'paddlings' produced only the occasional small chub, and by late afternoon I was convinced that all my mud-stirring wasn't really solving the problem. At the same time I felt almost sure my bait was lying in the correct spot – and equally sure that as darkness began to descend the bigger chub would begin to feed. But when the time arrived to pack up I still hadn't made contact.

Normally, I would seldom cast a bait into any area without first giving some thought as to why I was putting it there. I cannot think what prompted me to drop my crust-baited hook about a rod's length out opposite where I was sitting. I suppose it was a sort of hopeless, end-of-a-fruitless-day last cast. What I do know is I completely missed the first two savage bites and then netted a chub just under 4lb. This was followed by two more equally violent tugs which were missed, then a fish just less than 3lb and a couple around the 2lb mark.

By this time it was nearly dark and I had promised to be home early! With more than a mile to walk to the car and nearly 70 miles to drive I decided to go, but first there was something I simply had to find out. Removing the hook and lead I quickly slipped on a big float and tied a 'bomb' to the end of the line. With the light from my torch I plumbed the area in front and to right and left. This took longer than I thought but I consider my findings were well worth the effort.

Immediately to the left of the beck mouth and running out at right-angles to the bank was a spit of sand, the top of which was about 4ft below the surface. This ledge, which extended several yards out into the river, sloped away into a hole about 10ft in depth forming a *real* food trap. It was into this larder, which was almost opposite where I was sitting, that I had accidentally cast my bait.

The bed of the Ouse in this area is composed of loose sand and I imagine any heavy flood would regularly disperse the ledge I had found. But during a settled spell of the sort we had experienced for the ten days prior to my visit, then the push-out from the beck was obviously sufficient to cause a fresh, quick build-up. Of course the fish know all about this periodic food trap. Now, what's more, so do I!

Another trip to the Swale provided a further instance of fish feeding close in to the bank. The next time you are out river-fishing, count the number of anglers who are spending much of their time casting to the far side. True, there are times when it is both necessary and desirable to do this – crowded banks frequently cause fish to move across the river, and in clear, low water conditions the very act of casting will scatter fish so much that they have to be fished for at long range. And, of course, there are times when the best swim really is on the other side! But there are often just as many fish under your feet and by using a little common sense it is possible, and usually easier, to catch them at close quarters.

I remember leaving for the Swale soon after tea and arrived at my destination about 8pm. This gave me just about an hour to walk the banks and select a swim which I considered would give me a good chance of catching a decent chub. The spot I chose was a swim I had never fished before. Across the river was a row of willows, their branches dipping through the water surface. They looked 'chubby' and inviting but I knew I would get into a mess trying to drop a bait close to them after dark. Under my own bank the water ran at a fair pace and I judged it to be about 5ft deep and it was here I decided to fish.

Tackling up well back from the water's edge and keeping myself well down, I moved my gear quietly into position. A couple of swan shot on a sliding link held bottom nicely – but before starting to fish I dropped about a pound of broken-up sausage-meat into the swim. Until the light faded completely it was possible to hold the rod high and watch for bites on the tip outlined against the sky. After dark it was a simple matter to point the rod at the bait and feel for any bites.

The first fish, a small chub of about 1lb came within five minutes of making the first cast. It had picked up the bait lying no more than 2ft out from my own bank. In fact, of all the fish I caught before midnight not one came from more than a yard out.

At around 11pm I was beginning to wonder whether I ought to make a move. There were plenty of fish around but I appeared to have dropped among a pack of 'shoal' chub – fish weighing between 12oz and 2½lb. I had a dozen of them in the net along with a couple of typical Swale barbel around the 2lb mark. Then I hit a fish which set the clutch sizzling as the line tore off across the river. When I considered the fish had gone far enough I clamped down and leaned hard into it. Under the willows at the far side there was a flurry of white water and the line sang as I laid on more pressure. After two more short runs the fight was virtually over and I heaved a sigh of relief as I slid the net under a chub of 5lb 2oz, exactly 20 inches long.

By midnight I added eight more average-size chub to my keepnet. And then I hooked two eels with two consecutive casts, both on sausage-meat. So I baited up with cheese and blow me down if I didn't catch two more eels! I don't mind catching eels when I am fishing for them – but I cannot stand the sight of the things when I am trying to catch other species. I baited with crust, then flake, then paste. I didn't catch any more eels but neither did I get any more bites. So I unrolled my sleeping bag and put my head down for a snooze.

Next morning I caught only one more fish, a 2½lb barbel, and then set about the task of taking a few photographs before going home. I had promised to be back for breakfast and to take out my family and it's surprising how much time is involved in taking pictures of oneself.

Chub on floating crust

I can never lay down any hard and fast rules about getting chub to take crust off the top. On the river Bain you can sometimes spend hours, even days, without the fish showing any interest whatsoever and yet when they do they are invariably of better quality.

At the start of the season in 1963 I had taken along a large bag of crusts and I spent more than an hour sending them downstream on the surface. I had just about given up hope when, about 60 yards downstream, I spotted a swirl and one of the crusts disappeared. Inside 20 minutes I had two fish on the bank – a five pounder and one of 5lb 4oz.

The first time I ever saw this method tried successfully on the Bain was some years earlier when Reg Brotherton knocked out a couple of five pounders. Like the two I caught they were dark, not very attractive looking fish. I cannot account for this peculiar colouration.

It is really strange this business of chub taking floating crust. I have already mentioned when Reg caught them at the end of a winter's day on the upper Witham. There was another time when I was fishing on the Wye near Hereford with members of the Cormorants Angling Club. We had all spent much of the time, without much success, legering various baits and I decided to wander upstream taking with me a few crusts.

Above a bend I floated down a couple of pieces and they were both snapped up before they had travelled 10 yards. I hurried back for my tackle and in next to no time was catching chub while being watched by a gathering of passing Sunday strollers!

Bullocks to the rescue – 1962

You're never too old to learn is probably the moral behind an experience shared by Reg and I whilst fishing for chub on the Lincolnshire Bain. Actually the honours lie with Reg who, by taking advantage of a natural situation, saved what might well have been a very lean weekend – at least as far as fish catching was concerned.

We arrived on our stretch of the river to find the surface covered from bank to bank with blanket weed. Apart from small pockets of clear water this weed was so thick that I feel sure a cat could have crossed the river without getting wet. The small weirpool that I had fished at the end of the previous season was hardly recognisable. The pool had a lid of this damnable weed and the only clear area was at one end of the weir-sill, where the water trickled over into a shallow run that was full of small dace and roach.

We decided that perhaps the best method would be to work our way along the bank, casting a lobworm into the open spaces in the weed, and for three hours this was what we did. It worked fairly well too, for as darkness fell we had landed a number of chub but nothing larger than 3lb. These fish had been struck, bull-dozed out of their holes and over the top of the weed – all in one movement. Once a fish managed to get beneath these solid rafts of 'greenery' they invariably gained their freedom and several larger chub were lost in this manner.

The following morning at first light we each went our separate ways, arranging to meet for breakfast back in the bivouac area. It was as I returned to this spot that I noticed Reg coming downstream extremely pleased with himself. As we had breakfast he told me the story. Apparently he had walked upstream as far as the cow-drink, which lies at the top end of the fishery, and had cast a lob into the clear water. He had had no success and was preparing to make a move when the bullocks from a nearby field waded in the river to drink.

These beasts were actually standing in the water when Reg saw a good fish rise 'amongst their legs', and a quick cast brought an immediate response in the form of a chub just under 4lb. In a short space of time (in fact whilst the water had remained muddy) Reg had whipped out seven lusty club. As soon as the suspended silt had settled, however, the fish were no longer interested.

It is a well known fact that fish will often feed in cattle drinks after the bottom has been disturbed by animals drinking. In the past I have taken bream, roach, dace and trout from such places, but I cannot remember catching a decent chub amongst the commotion caused by cattle drinking. Many anglers will shy away from a cow-drink or complain bitterly when the animals wade in to quench their thirst but there are times, particularly during conditions of high summer and low water, when these four-footed, wallowing beasts might well save the day – as indeed they did on this occasion.

Slug 'em with a slug!

Let me say straight away that I'm sure we do not use slugs as often as we should. To date I have caught seven species of fish on them including bream, trout, perch, chub, roach, eels and, on one occasion, a barbel. Carp have also been caught on them, although not by myself.

Of the seven species mentioned my greatest experience is with the chub. I have caught scores of chub on slugs. These fish *love* slugs whether they are black, brown or white, small or large. Other fish might like to eat them as much, but I have never put in the concentrated effort of trying slugs with other species as I have with chub.

One problem with using slugs as bait is in having sufficient handy at the right time. If too many are kept in too small a container they are inclined to become sick and quickly die. To exploit the full potential of slugs I am sure that sufficient are needed to be able to bait up one's swim while fishing, as one would with any other bait. On a warm, wet night it is often possible to collect enough for fishing the following day from one's garden, or from any similar 'green' area. But I find the darn things are never out in the desired numbers at the times when I need them.

On still waters particularly I think it essential to have sufficient to be able to throw in a few loose ones from time to time as feed. I doubt whether many find their way naturally into still waters. Slugs are covered in a remarkably adhesive slime and they are not easily dislodged and washed in, even by the heaviest rain. On rivers the situation is somewhat different. After heavy rain or during flood conditions, slugs are washed into the water along with leaves and other debris to which they cling. Ditches and dried up stream beds usually contain a wealth of slug life and the first prolonged rain will flush many of them into the parent river. I find it significant that my best chub catches have been taken on a rising river.

On one particular all-night session in Yorkshire I crouched under my brolly while the rain poured down hour after hour. At around 2am I switched on my torch to tie on a fresh hook and found I was surrounded by an army of the most beautiful black slugs one could wish to see. Up to that point my fishing had been poor, but a switch to slug as bait brought a vicious bite at almost every cast.

I doubt whether colour matters much although I have only caught roach and bream on small white slugs. Chub will take any sort but prefer a good mouthful. I like to offer them a big black or brown one on a size 6 or 8 hook, but they will equally gobble up a bunch of smaller ones. They are a good bait in so much that they are soft and yet, at the same time, will not throw off the hook. Simply stick the point through the 'tail end' – the end opposite the horns!

A 7lb barbel I caught came as a complete surprise. After fishing with slugs in many swims that contained both chub and barbel but catching only the former, and from extensive 'negatives' on the subject from many other anglers, I had decided that barbel just did not eat slugs.

'Impossible' swims

Most chub fishermen know only too well the chub's fondness for some sort of cover. They particularly like a stretch where branches of bankside trees overhang the river. Usually the fish in such places are not difficult to catch providing you make a careful approach. If the chub are feeding, the choice of bait is not of great importance. I find that if they are unaware of my presence and are in a feeding mood, then a good mouthful of worm, bread or cheese is taken without any hesitation.

During the summer months it is often possible to wander along the bank hooking a fish below every suitable tree, but there are times when we reach a swim where we cannot present our tackle successfully for some reason. The most common hazard is when there is too *big* an overhang – where branches reach over and down *into* the water and so prevent our bait reaching the fish beneath.

Normally it is possible to cast to a spot opposite the swim and, by rod manipulation, coax the current into manoeuvring the bait into position, but there are times when the flow eases up *outside* the sheltering branches and even a bait on a floatless, leadless tackle refuses to enter the 'taking' area. I know that fish are often caught on the edge of their cover and if the bait is left in position long enough it will be taken in the end, usually by one of the smaller chub. Average sized shoal chub seem to be continually restless and are more liable to be found moving up and across the current or in and out from cover than are their larger brothers.

Bigger chub do, of course, emerge from their hideouts from time to time, to have a look round as it were, but apparently there is no set pattern as to when they will appear. It may be several times in an hour, or only once a day. From my observations I think that the larger the chub the wider spaced are its visits to the 'outside world'. All this creates problems when you are chub chasing and confronted with one of these 'impossible' swims. In the first place it's not always certain that there is a large chub present. Often the fish are out of sight among the roots, and it is difficult to know whether to place your bait on the 'outside' edge of the swim and hope for the best, or whether to by-pass these inaccessible places and move on to an easier spot.

Quite often you can send down a floating crust close to the bank and so avoid the obstruction. This will sometimes pay off, especially if a few loose pieces of bait are introduced from time to time. I find, however, that the larger chub, in these circumstances, are not always willing to rise to a floating bait, though they are eager to accept a crust lying on or near the bottom. There is a simple way to present such a bait and I first discovered it when tackling some barbel that were in a similar position. The idea is to select a piece of crust that is just – *and only just* – buoyant enough to float on the surface when carrying the weight suspended beneath. A quarter ounce Arlesey bomb will be carried by a large crust and seldom is there any need to use a bigger weight.

The weight is placed on the line about six inches from the hook – the distance depending on how far above the bottom you want the bait to rise. The crust, which just supports the weight, is swum down, and retained in position once it reaches the desired spot. When the crust becomes thoroughly soaked it will slowly begin to sink and settle nicely on the bottom just where it is wanted. This takes no more than a couple of minutes if the crust is properly matched with the weight. You will then be fishing a straightforward leger tackle in a spot that at first glance would have appeared impossible to reach.

Leaf-covered branches increase the dangers, but there are still plenty of apparently 'impossible' swims when only the bare twigs sweep the water. In summer or winter you can usually devise some way of getting bait to the fish, and trotting down a weighted crust is one of them.

My best Chub – 1963

In August 1963 I fished the upper Great Ouse as a guest of Dick Walker. I stayed in the comparative comfort of the fishing hut that had been built by Dick and the Taylor brothers. There were comfortable bunks, a well stocked larder and a supply of drinks all laid on for visitors.

I had fished the river on previous occasions, but only during the winter months, and I think anyone who is familiar with the territory will agree it had problems all its own during the summer months. Apart from the occasional small pool, the river becomes almost choked with aquatic vegetation, mostly of huge beds of bulrushes and water lilies. The margins too are thickly overgrown with reed and sedge. The river in summer becomes a series of channels winding their way between forests of lush summer growth, and catching chub from them demands a great deal of concentration.

The best approach, on any water of this nature, is to spend a certain amount of time trying to locate your fish before actually trying to catch them. This is what I mostly did on the first couple of days I was there. I spotted a lot of smaller chub and marked down a few better specimens that would weigh between three and possibly over six pounds. I saw one fish in the 'bream hole' which would weigh nearer 9lb.

Finally I was ready for my attack and went into action armed with a carp rod, 8lb line, hooks ranging in size from 10 to 2 and an assortment of baits that included lobworms, bread, sausage-meat, black slugs, cheese and a supply of crayfish that were hand-caught from the river.

The weather at the time was bright and sunny, and fishing was by no means easy. Although small chub up to a couple of pounds could be picked up during the day, the better fish were all taken in the early morning or after the sun had set.

The first three pounder came at about 5.30am. I was fishing a lump of cheese in a narrow neck of water that ran out from a shallow pool when I took this one. Later that same day, in fact after dark, I placed another chunk of cheese in the same spot, feeling for the bites by holding the line in my fingers. The bait had been in position about twenty minutes when I felt the line 'draw' slightly and then run rapidly through my fingers. I struck, leapt to my feet and, as I saw the rod double up in the pale light from the moon, I began to wonder whether I hadn't hooked the grandfather of all chub. However, it took but a few seconds to realise that I wasn't playing a chub but an eel which turned out to be a fish of majestic proportions. It weighed 4½lb, and I was thankful I had with me a large landing net.

Other chub in varying sizes followed during my stay,

among them a plump 4½lb fish that was hooked, played and landed in a patch of water a yard square on a line shorter than the length of the rod. A further three-pounder came from under a bush of loosetrife which overhung the water. But the fish of the week was one that I had seen on my earlier reconnaissance. It lived with three other chub in a gravel-bottomed swim surrounded by bulrushes. The smallest of the four fish weighed 3lb. I caught him on a piece of cheese and put it back half-a-mile higher upstream. The two 'middle' ones I guessed at about 4lb, and the fourth at well over five.

I tackled the five-pounder at the end of my stay. Some rain had arrived to colour the water and I fished the swim with the biggest lobworm I had in my tin, feeling all the time that if a bite did come it would be from one of the smaller fish.

Half an hour I waited while roach and dace tweaked the ends of the worm. Then, quite suddenly, the rod tip showed a more urgent dither and in a series of sharp pulls bent right over before I drove home the hook. The struggle was fierce but short lived. Several tackle-testing dashes were made for the bulrushes before I eventually slipped the net under a fat, 21 inch long chub which, when subsequently weighed, pulled the balance down to exactly 6lb.

Fred J. Taylor had said if I caught a chub over five pounds to give him a ring, so I carried the fish back nearly half-a-mile to the fishing hut, frequently 'dunking' it in the river en-route. After Fred had photographed the fish we returned it to the water in a pool opposite the hut.

There was a strange sequel to this story. Cormorant club member, Louie Thompson and her husband, Brian, fished the water about two weeks after my visit. Louie, fishing the same swim hooked, played and netted a fine chub of 6lb. Its length was exactly 21 inches. If it was the same fish, then it had piloted its way back through half-a-mile of lush summer growth of bulrushes, weedbeds and waterlilies!

Making the most of winter – 1962

All round anglers are never short of excuses to account for a fishless day. In summer we attribute the lack of bites to high temperatures, bright sunlight and the like; in winter the temperature is too low, the river too full, or an over-night frost has put the damper on sport. There are dozens of different excuses, many of them quite valid, but two particular incidents gave me cause for reflection on the vexed question of why fish refuse to feed.

The first occurred on the river Idle in Nottinghamshire when my club, the Cormorants, fished for the George Hallam cup – a trophy presented each season for the biggest roach caught. The morning of this competition was anything but encouraging. A week of mild weather had given way to a sharp overnight frost and no-one rated their chances very high. Nevertheless, with members spread out over two miles of water it was reasonable to expect that someone would be lucky enough to catch a fish or two.

The result, after four hours fishing, was two roach weighing 10oz and 6oz and one small chub. No one else had had a bite and, to a man, they were all prepared to swear that the sudden frost was responsible. We were in fact relieved to find this convenient loop-hole to slip through! But over complacency was short lived when we learned that two other fishermen fishing higher upstream had caught close on 40lb between them. Our only consolation then was that they had been fishing the deepest hole in the river and the fish had congregated there.

The second incident occurred when I paid a visit to a favourite 'chub run' on the river Wharfe in Yorkshire. Two days prior to my trip the first snow of the winter had fallen – and thawed – and after I had motored through thick frost I arrived to find the river bank-high and a chocolate brown. The temperature was 38°F and water was rushing through the 'chub run' at a great pace.

I decided to leger the run and let the bait work right in under the bank – a scheme which cost me eight leads! By 3.45pm my total catch was one small chub that had accepted a lobworm, and I was tempted to pack up, convinced that too many factors were against me.

My 'last cast' was with a piece of crust to an area of water on the far side of the river that on previous visits had been a large patch of dry sand. It was now covered with about two feet of comparatively slow water and, having cast into it, I sat frozen and uninterested, staring at the rod tip held at 90 degrees to keep the line free of the intervening current. Even when the rod first bobbed I only struck half-heartedly.

I was convinced that the 'bite' was the result of rubbish fouling the line, or a shifting lead. But all feeling of cold left me as I pulled a lively chub through the fast centre flow and slipped it into the net.

It was the first of five fish between 1lb and 3½lb landed in twenty minutes. The best one was netted in almost total darkness. The remainder, although not big, all gave me plenty to think about and I appreciated their last minute co-operation.

Many anglers maintain that winter fishing is not worth the discomfort that goes with it and I must confess that from the time I peered through the bedroom window at 5.30am on that frost-bound Sunday to the moment I hooked my first fish, I was almost prepared to share their view. But as I pulled those chub from the far side of the river through the speeding, churning current, and realised another problem had been solved, all thoughts of discomfort vanished.

I now know where fish can be expected on that stretch of the Wharfe under conditions that I might normally walk away from. I also know that had I not found those fish I would have returned home saying the conditions made fishing impossible!

PIKE

Spinners versus livebaits – 1959

The arguments as to the merits of the two most commonly used methods of catching pike (before deadbaiting became popular) is an old one. Some swear by spinning, others by livebaiting. I prefer to spin whenever I can. Whether it is the better method, I think, depends on the part of the country in which you live. In Lincolnshire, where I do the greater part of my pike fishing, I am certain that from, say, the end of November to March live-baiting would win hands down over spoons and plugs. But for the first eight weeks of the season I would put my money on the spinner, providing he knows the job!

Vast changes have taken place in Lincolnshire pike fishing since the end of the last war. I remember that if you saw a chap using spinning tackle before the war it was something to wonder at. What a difference today! On the many popular Lincolnshire waterways on any Sunday in October/November you can see anglers of all ages, from schoolboys to experienced adults, *all* trying to catch pike by spinning. The odd thing is that for the first couple of months of the winter season these anglers *do* catch pike – lots of pike. But come December there is a change. The spinners are shaking their heads in disappointment and the livebaiters are the only people catching fish. From then on to the season's end the men with the bungs reap the harvest.

I have a theory about this. At the start of the season the pike are gullible, slashing without caution at almost anything that is thrown at them. After the first few weeks of being caught and put back (the lucky ones!) they become wise about artificial lures, especially badly presented ones. I feel sure this is the main reason for the fall off.

If you fish these areas and want to catch pike throughout the season you cannot afford any scruples about using livebaits. If I fished in a less hard fished district I should fancy my chances equally well with my spoons and plugs, but for anyone who has qualms about livebaiting, here is a tip. Fish with a dead bait mounted on a spinning flight. A small roach or gudgeon so used will produce pike when all the metal or plastic baits have failed.

Perhaps even more deadly is a dead fish threaded on to a wire trace. Pass the trace through the eye of a baiting needle, then thread the wire in at the mouth of the bait and out at the vent. Tie on a treble hook and pull it back until the eye of the hook rests against the vent. At the other end of the trace, have a swivel to which is attached the line. So mounted, the bait has a nice slow spinning wobble which is often fatal to indifferent pike.

Once, in Lincolnshire, I was wobbling a dead bait while at least 20 others were using artificial lures. At the end of a hard day the spoons and plugs had not accounted for a single fish, though my two dead baits had taken two. Even the livebaiters had done very little, except one angler. Using small chub, a fish alien to the water, he caught 12 pike. The previous week he had landed a dozen fish – including one of 24lb – all on chub livebaits!

If your water is heavily fished for pike, put away your spinning tackle or change your tactics and use a mounted dead bait. Either that or forget your scruples about livebaiting and bring along a few fish which are alien to the water.

The Pike problem – 1959

I have included the following, as I wrote it in 1960, to highlight an issue that was then current. It is interesting to see how attitudes have modified since then. My fears for the pike's future clearly proved unfounded!

Three things prompted the writing of this article. The first was a letter to *Angling Times* by J.W. Smith, of Lincoln, condemning the ruthless killing of pike by Sheffield anglers in Lincolnshire waters. The second was extracts from *Fishing Notes* written by E. Jeffcock, the *Sheffield Star* angling reporter, advising the destruction of pike in all waters. And, lastly, the tremendous increase in pike fishermen over the preceding three or four seasons, and their general attitude towards the pike.

Let me deal with the last one first. The increase in the number of fishermen in the post war years had been enormous, and though trout, carp, barbel and other specialist anglers have increased considerably, pike hunters have shown a fantastic leap ahead of all the rest. Why?

Firstly, I think, the pike is such an accessible fish. Like the roach, it is widely distributed. Secondly, the cheaper fixed-spool reels and spinning rods, which could be bought on hire purchase, put pike spinning within reach of many more anglers. Thirdly, the publicity given to pike fishing in the angling press prompted every third angler to arm himself with pike tackle.

All this was good. I delight in seeing anglers enjoying the intricacies of working a spoon and the thrill of a tussle with a pike. But why knock each fish on the head? Why kick it to death as soon as it is landed, whatever its size?

To a newcomer to pike fishing even a three-pound fish looks big, and is so grand to show off to the neighbours! It is also said that pike are detrimental to other types of fishing and it is true that in a preserved water pike can be a nuisance. It is also true that in a small enclosed water, carp thrive better without pike than with them. But carp, in this country, are not likely to breed to the point of overcrowding. Otherwise, in a majority of coarse fish waters, pike are an asset.

Let me give three examples. In the Hampshire Avon game and coarse fish (including pike) are plentiful and grow to specimen size together. Hornsea Mere in Yorkshire holds big roach, perch *and* pike. And Slapton Ley is noted for its enormous rudd and its big pike.

Mr Jeffcock mentioned two places where he advised the killing of all pike – Chapel Hill and Sleaford Cut in Lincolnshire. Any angler who fished these waters regularly would admit that the quality of the roach had *increased*. Indeed, Mr Jeffcock himself told us what good roach were to be caught there almost every week of the season. But I had no doubt at all that the quality of these fish would have declined if all the pike were destroyed as he advocated. Perhaps Mr Jeffcock had read of the time when gamekeepers shot and displayed on their gibbets anything that flew and possessed a hooked beak. Subsequently, farmers were wringing their hands and wondering what to do about the hordes of wood pigeons raiding their crops. We shall be likewise wondering what to do with the shoals of *minute* roach in a few years time at Chapel Hill if the present slaughter of pike continues.

Lastly, I had much sympathy with Mr Smith. It was true that many Sheffield anglers were guilty of killing pike of 'any size' at that time, but not all of them were. Shortly before his letter appeared, while spinning in Lincolnshire, I caught and returned eight pike, and I knew of many anglers who would have done the same. But, to judge by letters in *Angling Times*, it appears that thoughtless killing of pike is practised widely.

Put the pike in its true perspective. It is a sporting fish. Return it to the water to continue its task of maintaining the balance of fish life. Unless something is done pretty quickly, the day will not be far distant when pike are as rare as powan and all our waters will be teeming with underfed, undersized and unwanted 'sprats'.

'Drain' Pike – 1960

Several years ago, whilst prospecting in the heart of Lincolnshire, friend Reg and I discovered a narrow drain on which we obtained permission to fish from the farmer owner. We were convinced he thought we were mad to fish in his land drain, for he obviously could hardly believe his eyes when, at the end of the day, we presented him with an 8lb pike.

Each winter we tried to make at least one visit to this distant water, and on every trip the little drain provided us with capital sport. The majority of the pike there are not big – they average between 3lb and 8lb – but they are plump, healthy fish, numerous and hard fighting. If we fancied a bit of fishing fun without working too hard for it and without overtaxing our brain power, the little Lincolnshire drain was the first place we thought of.

The drain had additional merit in that it contained at least one specimen around the twenty pound mark. On one of my visits I had a fish of this calibre thrashing under my rod point. I might have landed it too if it were not for the smaller pike which I had handled earlier on a tight line with the slipping clutch screwed up tight.

The clutch was still solid when I hit the much bigger fish, which immediately decided when it saw me to make a bolt. The result was I was left feeling rather sick and looking at a limp line hanging from the rod tip. Last winter Reg also made contact for a short time with what was probably the same fish, but we have not seen it since.

On a subsequent visit, armed with some small dead roach, I decided to commence operations at the extreme upper end of the drain, half a mile beyond the spot Reg had chosen to ply his spoons and plugs. I intended to work my way slowly down the water and meet Reg halfway, around lunch time. But one look at the water at the top end changed all that. I was dismayed to find it was barely 18 inches deep, clear and apparently fishless. So I worked my way back towards Reg much faster than I had intended, wobbling my dead roach bait as I went.

After about a quarter of a mile I had only one four-pounder to show, and Reg still did not seem to be anywhere in sight. I was puzzled – and still puzzled as I worked my way down to where he had settled down to start. Then, as I approached and watched him slip the net under a fat eight-pounder, I discovered the answer.

He was still fishing the first 80 yards of water and was having a real beanfeast. The pike had apparently accumulated in the deeper water there and he just could not go wrong. For an hour he had amused himself by going through his box and trying a variety of spoons and plugs in turn. Every one had lured a fish, and on two occasions he had been smashed by heavier-than-usual pike.

Whilst Reg had a breather – and a smoke – I took over, and after half-an-hour's hectic sport we broke off for lunch. In between sandwiches Reg told me that although the pike were prepared to take anything his better fish had been taken on a small silver spoon, which he proposed to use during the afternoon. I decided to do the opposite and chose a dull-looking, fish-shaped plug that my young daughter, Vanessa had bought me for Christmas. It took me quite a time to discover the best retrieving tactics for this particular lure and I settled eventually for a simple, slow winding of the handle. This proved to be the best, too, for after a quiet start I began to hook fish regularly and continued to do so until darkness forced me to stop.

Reg's afternoon experience with his silver spoon was interesting, especially during the last twenty minutes of the day when pike struck at his bait no less than fourteen times but still remained unhooked. When he changed, however, to a dark coloured plug he had two solid takes straight away. During the morning session, when the weather was calm and clear and a dull bait seemed the obvious choice, the pike preferred a flashy spoon. But from 2pm onwards, when heavy clouds pushed by a strong wind brought continuous rain – ideal one might think for a bright silvery lure – their tastes had changed and it was a dull bait that brought the best results. I wonder why?

Get the Pike at breakfast – 1960

In the late 1950s, I had been giving a lot of thought to the effect of water temperature on the feeding habits of pike. By 1960, however, I was formulating a theory that was rather different.

It is generally accepted that, when fishing during the winter, the most productive hours are those around midday. Most anglers have experienced the couple of hours around noon on a bitterly cold day when the fish have obliged for a brief spell.

It is almost certainly true that the chief cause of this break in the 'hunger strike' is a rise in the water temperature. This fact is so well known that most anglers hardly consider it worthwhile to be on the bankside at dawn during the real hard winter months: and they're probably right – in most cases. There is another theory that fish in cold weather digest their food much more slowly than in warmer temperatures. I'm not sure about this one. What I am sure of is that pike hunt their live prey by sight and to do this they need a certain amount of *light*.

However quick or slow their digestion, a winter's night from 4pm to 8am is a mighty long time for a scavenging pike to do without a bite. After sorting this out it seemed to me that *light rather than temperature* might govern the appetite of pike (and perhaps other sight hunting fish). Comparatively few anglers are out at dawn in winter to provide any conclusive evidence.

One particular incident seemed to support my theory that, whatever the temperature, pike would be looking for food as soon as the light became strong enough to see by. In 1958, an angler fishing in Lincolnshire had caught 147 pike in two days. I checked on this and discovered that all these fish were caught in the morning – *mostly before breakfast!*

On the first occasion Reg and I put this theory to the test we left home at 5am one morning early in March in a snowstorm! We reached the banks of a Lincolnshire drain as it began to get light and tackled up in the still heavily falling snow. The drain edges were frozen and the water temperature was just above freezing. A severe test this.

In just over an hour we had six pike out and lost another four. Shortly afterwards the snow ceased, the clouds rolled away and, almost miraculously, a brilliant sun shone from a blue sky. We caught no more pike.

Let me make it clear here that I have not said it is necessary to have a cold frosty morning to catch pike. On the contrary, a soft mild one would probably be more productive. What I do think is that the chances of catching pike are increased if one can be at the waterside when it begins to get light. I am aware that pike are caught on and off throughout the day but I believe that as the day becomes older the chances of catching pike (which have been filling their stomachs since dawn) begin to decrease.

Among the few anglers who are out at dawn in winter are the Taylor brothers and I discussed this theory with them. Their early morning piking had been confined mostly to Wooton lakes and usually with a dead bait laid on the bottom. Fred told me that their results were almost opposite to mine and that first light produced very little, while they caught pike in good numbers later in the morning.

There may be something in the fact that I was always fishing moving waters as against the still waters of a lake, but I hardly think so. More important is probably the fact that I was using a *moving* bait. In the half light of a winter's morning a dead bait lying on the bottom might not be so easy to see. Also, in conditions of low water temperature a pike might be loath to patrol far but quite willing to make a dash at a passing fish.

All this is supposition, but my experience last season has made me look forward with great interest to this coming one. As I have already said you can catch pike on and off all day, but I feel they might be similar to us humans. *Our* main big meal is our dinner with lesser meals and snacks in between. Whatever the water temperature I think the pike's big meal is his breakfast and as soon as it is light enough to see he will be looking for it.

Nessa's plug – 1950

One Christmas morning my ten-year-old daughter Vanessa entered my bedroom with her eyes twinkling mischievously and handed me my Christmas present, a bright new plug bait – much better than a tie or a pair of socks! It was a start-

111

lingly white plug with a greenish back, armed with two No 6 treble hooks. It was not what I personally would have termed a 'taking' plug. The colours didn't seem right: far too much white, I thought. Still, it might do for a dark day or dirty water. After a brief examination and a hug for Vanessa, I placed it in my bag along with my other lures.

Early in the New Year I found myself with a friend, Walter Taylor, on the banks of a small Lincolnshire drain. The main river, after heavy rain had washed in the Christmas snows, was swollen and running fast. In contrast, the drain was peacefully unaffected, lying between its high banks almost unruflled by the wind.

It was a warm wind, unnaturally warm for early January, and we perspired freely under our layers of winter clothing. The skies were overcast and conditions were just as I like them for pike fishing.

At about 11am my plug, which was twisting its way below a bed of loose-floating weed, stopped dead and my rod gave that delicious thump to which I responded likewise. The plug came back, a swirl in the weeds, and I had missed him. Out sailed the plug again and the same thing happened. After that it seemed the fish had had enough of me, so I called up Walt, who tried him with a spoon. The pike struck again after a few casts, and this time he was hooked. Walt played him out, gaffed him, removed the hooks from a nice six pound fish and we slid him back under the weed bed.

By midday I was still fishless, after trying various lures. Searching through my bag I spotted the brand new box containing 'Nessa's Plug' and decided, somewhat halfheartedly, to give it a trial.

On its first christening cast I observed two things. It was a *very slow* sinker and, when being retrieved, it came back without a flicker, looking extremely dead and 'artificial'. On the second cast I managed to impart a pretty roll into it by quick snatching turns on the reel. By the third cast I had got it rolling nicely, no more than three inches below the surface, but it still looked unreal. Much too white, I was thinking, when it was lifted clean into the air by a taking pike.

That fish was no more surprised than I was when I drove in the hooks! Walt arrived in time to see me slip back a plump seven-pounder. We then sat on the bank having a coffee and looking at the strange plug and discussing the mentality of the pike I had just returned.

Less than two hours later I had returned five more pike, all taking 'Nessa's Plug'! They were not big pike as pike go. I discovered later, in fact, that the previous autumn the drain had been pumped nearly dry, and all the large pike removed to the main river. Nevertheless, it has set me searching the tackle shops for a similar plug, and if I can get a deep sinking model, who knows what results I might have in those deep holes on the river.

There is a sequel to this. A few weeks later I was spinning for pike with 'Nessa's Plug' in holes in the weed-beds along the upper Great Ouse. A wayward cast landed the plug in a bed of bulrush, where it was firmly secured. No amount of pulling would release it from those tenacious stems and I finally, and very reluctantly, had to pull for a break. About an hour later and much further downstream I paused for a drink when Reg caught up with me. I related the sad tale about how I had lost my favourite plug and he offered me a consoling fill of tobacco from his pouch. When I opened it there inside, much to my joy, was 'Nessa's Plug'!

Apparently on his way downstream he had seen it swinging from the rush stem and, having with him a much stronger line than I had with me, had managed to hook it and haul it free!

On another occasion I remember over-casting on a small drain and solidly securing the plug into something on the opposite bank. Determined not to lose it I walked nearly a mile down the bank, crossed a narrow plank footbridge and then trudged back along the far side until I reached it.

More drain Pike – 1962

After two months of severe weather Reg and I, accompanied this time by Eric Hodson, set off to spend the last day of the season on a tiny Lincolnshire drain. We had decided in advance to cover the water with either spoons or plugs – a decision which was soon to be proved right, for my second cast produced a fish of 8lb.

My pike was scarcely on the bank when a call from Reg informed me that he too had hooked a fish – a nice perch –

and before he had landed it another shout from Eric told us that he had evened up the score by hooking a pike of similar weight to mine. A good start this. In less than ten minutes we each had a fair sized fish on the bank. Reg's perch, however, proved to be his only fish until late afternoon when he lifted out a small pike of 4lb. Meanwhile, Eric and I continued to catch pike at spasmodic intervals.

The fish were all retained in keepnets positioned at various points along the bank, the final tally of thirteen pike (Eric and myself taking six each) weighing a total of 86lb. Four of them were between 10lb and 11½lb, the largest one falling to my rod.

The catching of this particular pike was interesting in that I actually hooked and played it twice before landing it. At the time I was using a fish-shaped lure which, on the retrieve, I was able to observe as it rolled slowly through the water. As it did so the 11½lb pike slid out from under the bank and, with its nose only a couple of inches from the plug, followed it on its erratic journey. It followed the bait until the retrieve was almost over and then, just as the lure was rising towards the surface, the pike took a gentle hold and I struck. Not wishing to have a freshly-hooked fish thrashing about under the rod tip so early in the day, I allowed the fish to take a little line, but after a short struggle the plug shot from the fish's mouth and I was left staring at clouds of muddy water where the pike had disappeared under the far bank.

I made a mental note of the spot and some two hours later, after lunch, I carefully combed the area with the same lure. At the second cast the pike's snout appeared again and once more he followed the lure slowly and deliberately, this time it seemed with a little more respect, for he did not approach nearer than a couple of feet. This time, however, he did not take quite so gently. As the plug started to rise in the water, he made such a determined rush at it that I had difficulty in removing the bait which had lodged way back in the fish's throat.

Four more fish came unstuck during the day – why, I do not know, although I have my suspicions. I found that during casting the trebles on my fish-shaped lure – a very reliable 'killer', incidentally – tended at times to wrap around each other or to lodge themselves around either the link swivel or a part of the bait's anatomy – usually the tail.

If this occurred, and a pike grabbed the bait, the hooks failed to penetrate on the strike. Perhaps smaller trebles might have solved the problem.

Despite the misses we shared thirteen pike weighing 86lb – a highly satisfactory result after two months of near idleness. Little did we know, however, as we prepared to pack up, that disaster was only just around the corner.

Shortly after we arrived home we discovered that the ice which had covered our club pond since Christmas had melted and left tragedy in its wake. To our horror we found that very nearly our entire stock of carp and tench had perished and lay lifeless on top of the water. Splendid fish most of them were: fish we had nursed and tended over many years.

Lincolnshire fen drains – 1963

Fishing for pike increases with each year. It seems to hold a special fascination for younger anglers. Even a small fish of around five pounds looks big to someone only used to catching roach, perch, etc.

In certain parts of the country this increase in pike fishing brings with it the usual problem of too many anglers for too little water. Take Lincolnshire for instance. Until the start of the fifties you could safely say that the end of October would virtually see the end of fishing there (except for the few die-hard all-the-year anglers); but by the 1960s things had changed considerably.

Coaches and cars now left Sheffield and other places every weekend throughout the winter loaded with passengers bound for the fens in search of bream, roach and pike. Whatever the weather had to offer, be it snow, rain or gales, most Sundays would find the banks of the more popular places lined with anglers.

In the case of coach travellers they hadn't much choice of venue; they were dropped off at some well known destination and there they had to remain rubbing shoulders with other fishermen. But many anglers by then possessed their own transport and one would have thought that, with literally hundreds of miles of drains and waterways to explore, they would have thought twice before adding to the crowds at the more popular venues.

Pike fishermen, particularly, would do well to spend some of their time exploring the lesser waters of Lincolnshire. Fishing for bream (and to some extent roach) on these small waters in winter is a hit and miss affair and hardly worth pursuing but pike fishing, when conditions are right, can be most rewarding. There is not much point in fishing these drains until there have been a few frosts to clear away the weeds – which in summer often stretch from bank to bank. But once the weeds have gone then the angler is at liberty to spin, use a livebait or leger a dead fish as his fancy takes him.

These drains are ideal for the light spinning enthusiast, for though the pike are often plentiful their average size is not exceptionally large – although I have taken plenty of doubles with a couple of low twenties among them.

I say pike-holding drains because not all of them contain these fish, at least not in numbers worth pursuing. It is a case of trial and error. Given reasonable conditions the fish are not difficult to catch. I remember one drain when Reg and I amused ourselves by systematically going through our box of lures and hooking a pike on almost every spoon and plug we possessed. Of course fishing being what it is sport isn't always so fast and furious. In fact, a further visit to the same water failed to produce a single fish!

Contrary to what would be expected on such shallow waters we have found that the weather does not influence the pike's appetite. We have caught them in driving rain, snowstorms, high winds, bright sunshine and even when the drain edges have been fringed with ice. The greatest governing factor on your sport appears to be the height of the water. If the waterway is full then usually the pike are willing to feed, but a day of low water levels invariably brings patchy sport.

Unless a fish was required for eating we returned all we caught; after all, wholesale slaughter on these little drains would quickly denude them of their population.

There is one important thing to remember. The majority of these little drains are not 'club owned' and permission must be sought from the riparian owner before starting. Usually the owner is a farmer and permission is seldom refused.

Hornsea Mere

The fishing potential of this great mere first came to light during the years of the First World War. Large fish of several species were caught at this time including perch, pike and roach. It was, however, the catches of the latter which fired the imagination of the angling world. Roach of enormous size fell to the rods of such renowned anglers as Wilf Cutting, who held the roach record for many years with a fish of 3lb 10oz, and Jim Bazley, a brilliant all-rounder who won the 'All England' championship on two occasions.

There were many outstanding roach catches including one of 61 fish totalling 123lb which was taken by two anglers in one day, the bag being boosted by several fish over two pounds.

As well as his record fish, Wilf Cutting took another brace of roach weighing over 3lb at one sitting, and Jim Bazley, using a trace with two hooks, twice landed a couple of two-pounders at the same time, in a haul of over fifty of that coverted weight in one month. It is interesting to note that most of these fish were caught on a size 6 or 7 hook with a big lobworm as bait!

However, it is not the mere's roach that I am familiar with but its pike. In the early sixties those two fine anglers, Ray Webb and John Neville began to tackle the water's pike population. Big pike had been caught there before but never in quantity. Those two East Yorkshire stalwarts, Charles Derrick and Roy Shaw had taken some nice fish, but it was Neville and Webb who really put the mere on the map. They spent many days in their efforts to pinpoint the best areas, only catching the occasional fish, but when they finally began to get results they very wisely kept them to themselves.

They made some remarkable catches including, during a two day stint at the end of the 1964 season, a total of 22 pike weighing 219lb, with the best fish a twenty-pounder. Several fish were hooked and lost so no one could guess what the final tally *might* have been. But eventually they informed a few friends, including myself, and the memories of those days spent with John and Ray, and later with various members of the Northern Specimen Hunters Group, will always be remembered. Some of them I will relate here.

Hornsea Memories – 1964

Here again I have included a piece as it was written at the time. I find it interesting to look back and recall the sorts of problems that were taxing our ingenuity at the time. It is also worthwhile in providing a context for the developments in angling technique in more recent years.

If we examine the methods used for pike fishing up to the mid 1960s, we shall find that over the previous half century there has been little change. The deadbait-on-the-bottom method, introduced by the Taylor brothers, being perhaps the only exception.

This style of angling has now become firmly established, but it has brought with it its own particular problems. There is now little doubt that the pike, on most waters, is a confirmed scavenger and it will soon come to take a herring fished on the bottom. There is no problem there. Where the difficulty starts is knowing exactly when to strike.

The usual rig of most anglers is that of two treble hooks on a wire trace, the 'point' hook being attached near the bait's head, and the other halfway down the body. A couple of turns of cotton secures the trace at the tail. This is probably as good a terminal tackle as has yet been devised, but in my experience it has its shortcomings in that one can never guarantee that a pike will be cleanly hooked.

This is what usually happens: after the bait has been picked up the pike is allowed to move off; it stops, turns the bait, begins to 'run' again – and a strike is made. However, such a procedure is by no means foolproof. Even after a run of 50 yards or more it has been known for a pike to eject the bait on the strike; additionally there are numerous occasions when the herring is swallowed, making it almost impossible for the angler to remove the hooks.

Some while back I concluded that a rig was necessary which would enable the angler to strike immediatley the first run began – as one does when carp fishing – and I was interested to read D.L. Steuart's article (*Fishing* magazine, November 1964) and find that he had been working on a rig very similar to one I had been trying myself.

We both used two lengths of wire trace secured to a swivel at the end of the line, but whereas Dave festooned his with hooks, I simply used two: one on each of the trace ends. These were stuck in opposite sides of the bait, about halfway down, and a tie of cotton neatly secures the two wires at the tail. If the pike picks up the bait sideways, as it invariably does with an offering the size of herring, then it almost certainly has at least one treble (more probably two) in its mouth and the strike is made as soon as the line starts to run out.

So much, then, for deadbaiting. Let us now look at live-baiting. Apart from the change from rigid rods to more supple ones, this method has altered little since the days of our forefathers, though with small baits there is a tendency to use a single large hook, or just one treble, rather than the usual snap tackle. This season, together with John Neville and Ray Webb, I have been trying out what is to us a new approach. It is simple enough, and has to date produced very satisfying results, but as yet a longer trial period is necessary before it can be truly assessed.

One of the biggest problems with livebaiting is that of obtaining baits, and if our experiments have been cur-tailed, it is because we have been trying to get baits small enough. One of the many angling theories is that a pike becomes suspicious because of the unnatural movements caused by the bait being tethered. It is suggested that the pike picks up 'distress' vibrations on its lateral line. Working on this theory I have simply lip-hooked two small fish on a single treble (gudgeon are ideal, but any fish not more than 3 inches long will do) in the belief that not just one but two sets of vibrations will be 'beamed' out. Whenever we have managed to collect livebaits small enough, we have had successes which encourage us to pursue the idea.

Boats and strange baits – 1962

With the inevitable disturbance that goes with messing about in boats it would appear sensible to cast out a bait a fair distance. However, one incident I recall may serve to illustrate that, as with many other sorts of angling, one can often cast *too far*.

I had manoeuvred my boat into position and after lower-ing the anchor had generally fiddled about with tackle and stuff without much concern for absolute quiet. The main object of the exercise was to try out some varied pike rigs in conjunction with a variety of dead baits. In any case I did not anticipate any pike being in that particular area until much later in the day.

I had prepared a good sized mackerel and was dangling it over the side of the boat to see whether the float I was using could support it when out from beneath the boat shot a pike which pounced on the dead bait like a tiger. I was so surprised that I almost forgot to release the float which I was still holding in my hand.

Generally speaking I believe fish have little fear of boats and when disturbance is kept to a minimum many species actually use the shelter they provide out of choice. They may find a sense of security similar to that provided by a raft of weed. Pike probably find the darkness provided by the hull to be a good place to wait in ambush.

Over the years I have caught or seen caught quite a lot of pike on baits fished alongside boats. When the pike are actively on the rampage then even noise appears to have no effect on their relentless mission.

I remember one occasion when I was fishing with Ray Webb and John Neville. The pike were feeding well and while John was playing a fish and Ray was waiting to use the landing net, I was adjusting the camera to get off a few shots. We had long since thrown caution to the winds and at the time all three of us were standing bolt upright in the boat – enough to frighten away any self-respecting fish for miles.

Suddenly Ray shouted, 'Just look at that!' Earlier in the day a herring had come adrift and dropped over the side, where it had remained plainly visible at the bottom of four feet of clear water. Ray's exclamation was to draw our attention to a hefty pike which purposefully swam in and lifted the fish from under our very noses.

On a few occasions at Hornsea Mere I've witnessed pike snatch a bait tackle which has been brought in out of the way while another fish was being played and left lying down the side of the boat.

There was another time when a companion and myself had boated half-a-dozen pike when we were joined by Roy Shaw who came along to take a few pictures. He tied up alongside and while waiting for some action dropped a herring bait about a rod's length from the boats on his side. Almost immediately he had a run and landed a 17lb fish.

If two rods are being used it can be a good idea, from time to time, to place one bait just a few feet out. You may find it produces as many runs as the bait fished farther out.

Turning to the bait itself, I am a great believer in using pike baits which are alien to the water being fished. I am told that there are some waters where pike will not accept a dead bait – I'm thinking particularly of herrings, the most commonly used. Certainly, evidence shows that on some fisheries they have been weaned, by frequent exposure, into searching for and picking up herrings. It is also apparent that on waters where pike are frequently taken on herrings and returned, they become more and more difficult to catch on this bait. But a change to a different bait can produce results again.

There are many experiments one can try with a variety of sea fish which are comparatively easy to obtain. Mackerel are a vogue but there are plenty of others you can use, particularly if you are interested in using an outsize dead bait.

I know an angler who spent several weekends trying to catch a chub of about 3lb to use as dead bait for pike. He particularly wanted a chub because it was a species foreign to the water he was to fish. Why he didn't save himself all that trouble and buy a 3lb codling from the fishmongers I shall never know. I'm sure it would have worked just as well. Of course buying sea fish of 3lb-4lb in weight could add to your weekend anlging expenses, but you won't require more than two fish of such calibre and they are about equal to the cost of a dozen or so herrings.

If outsize baits have never been used on your water then it is worthwhile taking one along just to see the reaction – both from the pike and from other people!

On one outing, a becalmed yacht came drifting by as I was retrieving my bait – a mackerel of near specimen size. Seeing the fish break surface the conversation between myself and one of the crew went as follows. "You've caught one then!" "No, this is the bait." There was a pronounced silence followed by: "You're after pike then. You'll be lucky to catch one big enough to take that." "I can sit here all day and not catch a little pike. I might just as well sit here and not catch a big 'un!" was my reply.

The 'Hornsea' Pike rod

At about the height of the pike catching period at Hornsea I was developing a new pike rod. It was made from hollow glass fibre and was eventually named 'The Hornsea' and was marketed by Sportex Fishing Tackle Co of Sheffield. It was a time when herrings, fished mainly on the bottom, were taking 99 per cent of the Mere's fish. The prototype made several trips to the Mere and I remember one occasion when Charlie Derrick telephoned to say he would join me around two o'clock in the afternoon and that he would be bringing along some dace livebaits.

I was afloat at first light and had tied up the boat at a spot where I could fish two baits into the sanctuary, an area where boats were not allowed to enter.

Herrings were undoubtedly the bait to use. The previous season the Northern Specimen Hunters Group members had taken a total of 203 pike (88 of those were more than 10lb) on herring and the season in question, 1967, had started where it had left off.

When Charlie joined me after lunch I hadn't had a single run and he enquired whether I would like one of his dace livebaits. I thanked him but remarked it would only be a matter of time before I started catching.

After tackling up he dropped a bait over the side and almost immediately his bung disappeared. He eventually boated a nice fish just into double figures! "Did I want a dace?" he enquired. "No," I replied, "it's only a matter of time now." Ten minutes later he netted another fish of 14lb and still I refused his offer of a livebait. But when his third fish of 16½lb was landed half an hour later and I still had not had a run, I couldn't get a dace on fast enough.

I took two doubles in quick time; Charlie boated a fourth fish and then it was all over. But had he not been there I would probably have fished the day out convinced I had no pike in the area. And also the 'Hornsea' pike rod would not have had its mettle tested!

Deadbaits and Pike that take too well

In spite of the good numbers of pike that were being caught during the sixties there arose a worrying problem about halfway through the decade. The worry was the number of deeply-hooked fish we were catching on legered herring. Frequently the hook was way down in the stomach of the pike. As could be imagined innumerable variations were tried to overcome the problem, without much success.

When the hooks were swallowed so deep that they could not be removed without injury we did what we considered best under the circumstances, that was to cut the trace as near to the hooks as possible. How much or to what extent this inconvenienced the pike was difficult to determine. At worse it could bring about a lingering death; at best, a hook lodged in the lining of the gut cannot do the fish any good. But both myself and other anglers had opened healthy fish and found treble hooks in the last stages of corrosion. Obviously the pike's digestive juices are pretty potent.

At the time people wrote in the angling press telling us how they struck and always hooked their fish in the mouth. At the time because of the intense seven-day-a-week that was taking place at Hornsea, 'text-book-type' runs, although they still occurred, the subsequent strike, following the accepted pattern, rarely produced pike hooked in the same manner.

If I could go into this more deeply: a pike picks up the herring, moves off with it, stops to turn it and then runs off a second time. If we work by the book we should time our strike to coincide with the second run.

What could happen at Hornsea was as follows. The first run-off could be anything from a few feet to 80 yards or more. The angler would strike as the second line movement began, hook the fish and land it. Then, in most cases, he would find he required a pair of extremely long-handled pliers – and if he was lucky he could retrieve the hooks. On almost an equal number of occasions he would find that the fish, even after nearly emptying his spool, had dropped the bait or was so lightly hooked that it shed the tackle after a short space of time.

We also experienced a number of unconventional runs when only a short length of line was peeled from the spool. The run stopped and after a period of time the line was wound in only to discover a fish on the end – one that had gorged the hooks. What was more alarming was on other occasions when we wound in the bait – having seen no indication of a take – to find a fish on . . . with the herring deeply buried in its gut. This latter sometimes happened when using a float for better bite indication.

We devised many kinds of tackle to try to avoid this sort of thing, without success. I made up a double trace rig with a hook on each end. These were stuck one in each side of the herring on the assumption that if I struck the fish on its initial run – if it made one! – I would have a fair chance of hooking it in the jaw. When the first run developed I struck before the fish had gone three feet. I hooked it, right enough, but this time both hooks were out of reach and irretrievable in the pike's stomach.

Large single hooks, although easier to remove than trebles, were not the answer to these 'unorthodox' pike. Damage to the fish was still inevitable if the hooks had to be dug out from inside the fish. As for the timing of the strike, we varied it through all stages of the run, and although one particular instance might produce a jaw-hooked fish it was just as likely that the next half dozen would require remedial action with a long disgorger.

Following the incident with Charlie Derrick more anglers started to use livebait, but overall Hornsea pike still preferred herring in spite of the 'evidence'. On one visit four companions and myself boated 13 fish weighing 190lb, while seven other anglers, all using livebait, didn't have a single run between them.

Towards the end of the sixties pike catches noticibly dropped and it was my belief that this lack of sport was brought about for several reasons: (a) a check I made towards the end of the decade revealed that something approaching one thousand herrings per week were being thrown into the Mere as 'groundbait' or discarded at the end of a day's fishing; (b) because many of the large pike, which had been gorged and had been returned to the water, had died – Charlie, on one occasion when the water was clear, spotted numerous double figure dead pike lying on the bottom; (c) quite a number of fish were killed and taken home; (d) the few large pike which did remain had an endless larder of free offerings and therefore the chance of one of them picking up the angler's bait became less likely, and (e) most of those lucky remaining double-figure fish had been hooked so often that they began to treat herrings – and any other bait – with the utmost suspicion.

The saturation 'feeding' undoubtedly accounted for the fish that were found to be deeply hooked without giving any sign of a run. With such a spread of loose offerings there was little need for them to pick up a bait and bolt. Further to this many fish became crafty and it became not unusual to retrieve a bait to find it sliced by a pike's teeth, having been picked up by a fish obviously suspicious of the trebles.

I became so sickened by the sight of deeply hooked fish that I virtually stopped legering deadbaits on waters that are heavily fished for pike. Whenever I do resort to legering I use a rig I have simplified as follows: a single, size 6, eyed hook is slid on the trace and one treble is tied on the end. One point of the treble is stuck into the head of the bait somewhere around the gill cover. The single hook is put through the tail, simply to secure the bait during casting.

Within seconds of the first run coming to an end I tighten on to the fish and strike on the assumption that if the pike is worth catching it will, at this point, have turned the bait and at least have the head in its mouth. Should I fail to connect then I have developed a philosophical attitude that the pike was too small to be worth catching anyway!

SPECIMEN GRAYLING – 1962

How does one catch a specimen grayling – are there any anglers in the country who specialise in the taking of out-size members of the *Thymallus* tribe? There are *all round* specimen hunters and anglers who are expert at catching large fish of individual species, but who knows how to catch a big grayling with any consistency? Is it possible?

A 2lb grayling is a good fish on any water. Around my own city of Sheffield such a specimen would be treasured almost as much as a roach of equal weight. I have not compared seasonal returns, but I would bet the list of 2lb roach is higher than that of grayling.

In the hunting and catching of specimen fish there are certain rules laid down which act as a basic guide. First find your fish; don't scare 'em; correct tackle and, generally speaking, big baits for big fish. With these basic principles, plus a little common sense, one can usually come to grips with fish that go a bit above average in weight.

Many years ago after some success with various other species I decided to apply the same tactics to grayling. I chose a stretch of the river Dove that I knew from previous experience held some good fish. Instead of the usual trotting style I employed a light leger rig, baiting the hook with the thick tail of a big lobworm.

I caught one fish that day and was delighted, it was the best grayling I had ever caught, weighing a little under 2lb. At the time I was convinced that I had the answer – the big bait for big fish theory apparently worked with grayling as with most other species.

But since that first success many fruitless days have been spent using the same method and with it I have never taken another grayling of such proportions. It would appear that there is no cut and dried method for catching extra large grayling, and that it is a simple case of elimination. Once a shoal of fish is located the well-tried maggot or worm-trotting technique will catch the bigger as well as the smaller grayling – the junior fish usually surrendering first.

But what about the really monstrous grayling? If we are to

accept the record rod-caught fish which weighed 7lb 2oz (as at the time of writing but now thrown out, which in my opinion is a pity), then surely we can expect a number of 4 pounders to be swimming around somewhere. And if you examine the grayling returns for the past fifty years a *4lb* fish is a *monster*. Do these fish lead a life far different from the normal shoal fish. Have they developed special feeding habits that have yet to be discovered? Do they inhabit parts of the river where we would least expect them?

Some information regarding the accepted record fish would be interesting. Try as I might I can never obtain the *full* facts of its capture, just the usual details: weight, where caught and name of captor. That is until I had a long discussion with the late Tim Wilson of Skipton while we were fishing on the river Aire one winter for chub. Tim had actually seen a photograph of the fish which was caught by John Stewart from the river Melgum on 16 July 1949. Its length was 28½ inches. Sadly the photograph was of such poor quality it would not reproduce, but Tim said there was no doubt it was a grayling.

Tim also showed no surprise at its weight. On his favourite Aire in Spring he had observed grayling that were spawning and amongst them were fish he estimated to be in the region of five to six pounds – remember Tim was no stranger to big grayling, he had himself taken a fish of 4lb 12oz when he was twelve years old. Had he known at the time, it would have been a new record.

There was another grayling of 5½lb caught from the river Nith. It was witnessed by one of Tim's friends but was never recorded in print. It was landed by a visiting salmon angler who took it on a blue and silver devon minnow.

Years ago, both on the middle stretches of the Wharfe and on the Ribble, some massive grayling were watched spawning, one with a length judged by several anglers to be 30 inches and estimated to be in the region of 9 to 10lb. After spawning these giant fish seemed to disappear, mostly never seen again until the following spawning session. Except, on one occasion during late summer when Tim spotted a trio of five pounders rounding up and feeding on shoals of minnows.

The 'record' grayling was caught in July – not a time one would normally fish for grayling – but on more than one trip I have picked up the odd fish when I have been fishing for something else during the summer and they have invariably been full of little black snails. Grayling have been taken on hemp seed and I have often thought on these occasions, when snails are thick on the ground, the angler with a supply of hemp handy might well take a bag of fish to remember.

Pegged down for Grayling – 1964

The methods employed when bait fishing for grayling have changed little since angling for these fish first began. During the past few years a fresh look has been taken at the design of the grayling float, but by and large the old fashioned 'bob' still holds favour. Indeed, in the North at least, there is little one can tell the grayling expert about catching these delightful fish and, as his catches are usually quite good, it might appear somewhat presumptious of me to suggest that he tries a fresh approach. But let us have a look at the routine of the average angler after winter grayling.

More often than not, where space allows, he adopts a roaming technique. It is a common sight to see the Yorkshire grayling-angler walking the banks with a bag of maggots or worms slung around his neck, looking for the next likely swim. He seldom carries a keepnet, for he returns most of the fish as they are caught, perhaps keeping the occasional bigger one for the pan.

But why, I ask myself, does he spend so much time wandering? After all, grayling are shoal fish; frequently large numbers of fish are found together. Why not, then, stay put in one spot and try to take a good bag of fish without moving so much? Put this point to our average grayling angler and he will usually reply either that he moves when he has fished out the swim (meaning that he has caught most of the fish in it), or when no more bites are forthcoming, generally due, he will add, to the disturbance caused by the landing of two or three fish.

I will come back to this point later, but first let me say that I realise that some waters, especially the small, clear streams, will often produce most fish to the roaming angler. However, even on these a change from the usual tackle and methods can cut down the amount of searching and still put plenty of fish in the net.

I shall never forget when I was due to catch some grayling for a series I did for Yorkshire Television (in the days of black and white pictures). I obtained permission to fish on Pickering Beck, a narrow and clear stream in North Yorkshire. The crew were due to arrive on a Monday morning, so I went up on the Sunday and spent a few hours roaming the banks.

I spotted a shoal of fish and at the end of the day deposited into the swim nearly two pints of maggots. When the team had sorted themselves out I started to fish and during filming, which lasted on and off for several hours, I caught and retained in a keepnet fifty or more grayling, all taken from the same swim. It was almost impossible to scare those grayling in spite of the efforts of a wonderful cameraman, Charles Flynn, who not only entered the water just below the shoal and took pictures but also climbed a tree just above the fish dragging his camera with him.

I just quote this incident to show that even on a small, clear stream it is possible to net a good bag of fish without moving along the bank. It was difficult, as I have found on other occasions, to frighten a shoal of feeding grayling. There were times during filming when I couldn't get a good 'trot' down the swim for the cameraman to pick up the float, as bites were coming as soon as I lowered my tackle into the water.

But to continue. One winter I devoted a lot of time to grayling. I tried out several new ideas – at least they were new to me. Although I did not catch the specimens I was after, I did discover a few things which helped me catch more grayling than I had done previously with the accepted methods.

In normal water conditions grayling have a great liking for fast, bubbly, fairly shallow, runs and it was for such water that the 'bob' float was designed. Its fat, egg-shaped body grips the water wonderfully well and it rides the waves solidly as it hurtles down a rough swim, but I had never been very happy about the 'wake' caused by its body on the retrieve.

I knew, of course, that grayling were caught despite this, but I decided that even more fish would be netted if this unnatural disturbance could be ministered. This brings me back to our friend who claims either to have fished out his swim or to have upset the shoal by the playing of fish. In many cases I feel certain that the shoal is unsettled *not* by the splashing of a hooked fish, but by the continual 'wash' created by the float as it is brought back.

But to get back to my experiments. In choppy swims, where the water was deep enough for a float with a longer stem to be used, I tried porcupine quills of various lengths on top of which I fixed a float vane to aid visibility. Correctly shotted, these floats rode the water well and responded more decisively to a taking fish than did the conventional grayling 'bob' and, more important, the disturbance while being retrieved was cut by 50 per cent.

For use in extremely shallow swims – where a long-bodied float is too deep to be practical – I now use an excellent float put together by Eric Horsfall-Turner. This is a cigar-shaped cork, built on to a balsa or cane stem about 3in long. Their torpedo 'build' sets up little resistance and causes far less drag than the ordinary grayling 'bob'.

However, all grayling are not confined to 'typical' grayling water, and the long churning glides, 3-5ft deep, often hold their quota of fish. I now fish such swims exactly as if I were fishing for roach, with exactly the same sort of tackle and tactics. Grayling can be enticed from a long way downstream by the steady introduction of maggots, though the average grayling fisherman moves if no bites are forthcoming in the first fifteen minutes. To emphasise my point, I can remember several occasions when it has taken an hour or more before my regular trickle of maggots has brought a feeding shoal into range.

One last point. There are occasions when it is necessary to move, and occasions when, due to awkward banks, one has to wade. For such circumstances I made a bait apron. This ties around the waist and has two pockets; one carries a supply of maggots, the other a stock of worms. The polythene bags lightly tacked into each pocket can be renewed easily should they become messy, and it is a simple matter to empty them of their contents at the end of the day.

Driffield Beck Grayling – 1963

I have written before about the problems I have found when trying to catch better quality grayling. On the majority of waters I fish a pounder is an exceptionally good specimen, a two pounder extemely rare. No special tactics are needed to catch the heavier fish – where they exist – and it is usually a case of locating a shoal and eliminating the smaller grayling until the bigger fish come to the net.

Seldom do I get the opportunity to fish a water that holds a head of better-than-average grayling, so it was with eager anticipation that Reg Brotherton and I set off recently to fish a preserved beat on Driffield Beck in East Yorkshire. The Beck is, I believe, the only chalk stream in our part of the world and it grows not only some excellent grayling but also trout, pike and chub. Oddly enough its roach population only seem to grow to a moderate size.

However, we left home on a Saturday morning having booked ourselves in for bed and breakfast at a village pub near the fishery. We arrived at lunchtime and shortly after went along to view the river. The farmer/owner, whom we met on the bank, dampened our spirits somewhat by informing us that we had chosen an unfortunate weekend. It seemed that twice a year weed cutting was carried out higher upstream and our visit had coincided with the second operation!

Deciding to make the best of a bad job, we were soon tackled up and fishing and for the first hour we caught grayling (and roach) fairly steadily. The grayling averaged a good half pound with the occasional fish just topping the pound mark. After the first hour *sensible* fishing became pretty hopeless: the weed rafts became more dense and at times completely covered the river from bank to bank. By dusk we gave it up as a bad job and could only hope there would be some improvement the following morning.

But there wasn't. In fact the situation worsened as the day wore on. It was most annoying because the grayling in the swims we fished were prepared to feed; whenever a bait could be swum down to them without the tackle being fouled by weed we would get a bite.

We spent some time exploring the water with a view to a further visit, and managed to spot some fine grayling in the region of 3lb. Reg in fact managed to hook one but lost it after it became enmeshed in a mass of weed. The best fish of the weekend, which fell to my rod, weighed 1½lb.

An interesting event on the trip was a visit by East Yorkshire River Board bailiff, Stan Metcalf, who took us along to see a chub he had caught some months previously. He had returned this fish (about 3½lb) to a shallow stretch of the river overhung by a willow tree, and from that time both Stan and the local farmer had fed it daily on bits of bread.

This remarkable situation was made even more peculiar by the fact that in the meantime this fish had been caught on many occasions, on bread. In fact, the week before, a visiting lady angler had netted and returned it twice in the same day. Yet, despite this, the fish was still swimming around in the evening waiting for someone to throw it a piece of bread!

Furthermore, this very odd chub appeared to have had the power of transferring its strange behaviour to other species. Stan told us that for a week or more a half-pound grayling and a trout of similar weight had been in attendance, following the chub round the swim and racing it to any morsel that was tossed into the water.

If we returned again to this fishery we should ensure that weed cutting was not taking place. But this trip was by no means wasted. There *is* more to fishing than catching fish, and that chub certainly gave us food for thought.

Spinning for Grayling – 1967

Further downstream, where the Beck becomes the river Hull, there is more grayling fishing but the fish are not as thick on the ground as they are higher upstream. In November 1967 15-year-old Stephen Crane wrote to tell me that he and his father had observed one or two hefty grayling while fishing the Hull, but not a single fish had fallen to the usual methods of either fly or maggot trotted baits.

One afternoon Stephen decided to fix up a small spinner after a large trout he had spotted had refused all other baits. But the fish which took the spoon was not a trout but a fine grayling weighing three pounds. Since then he had taken three other grayling weighing well over the pound mark and all by spinning a small spoon.

When I joined Stephen recently I decided, because drifting weed made spinning a difficult poroblem, to fish the area using conventional tactics. It was a long, cold day with a biting east wind and not a sign of a fish did we see. But knowing from experience that grayling will often feed in the fading light, even on the coldest of days, I suggested we carry on until darkness.

Towards the end of the day I noticed a fish 'hump' the surface well down the swim. Quickly retrieving my tackle, I pushed all the shot up the line. This allowed the bait to swing up in the water each time I checked the float. About two thirds of the way down the swim the float slid under and, after a tidy scrap, I netted a 16 inch long grayling weighing 1lb 2oz. A few minutes later I repeated the performance with another fish of exactly the same proportions.

These two were the only fish of the day, but I learned a lot from this visit. On a future trip, when there is less weed about, I shall adopt different tactics. I intend to have ready a separate set of spinning tackle already rigged with a tiny spoon. Should the grayling show any response to normal fishing methods I shall put aside my float tackle and run a spinner through the swim. It is not easy to change over from a method which is successfully catching fish to try something else. But in view of Stephen's previous experience I might contact the bigger grayling which are present.

I brought home one of the fish both to eat and to examine the stomach content. The results of the latter were interesting. Throughout the day I had been feeding the swim with a steady trickle of maggots, red worms and brandlings. The maggots were multi-coloured from natural 'white' through to red, including various shades of yellow, orange and pink. The fish had eaten a considerable quantity of white and yellow, but not a single one of any other colour, neither had it eaten a solitary worm. An interesting example of pre-occupation, and I would have thought proof that fish can distinguish one shade from another.

Footnote: I subsequently fished tiny spinners for grayling and caught plenty of fish, but my hopes that it would prove to be a method which would sort out the 'men from the boys' didn't work out. It catches small grayling far quicker than it does big ones.

Fishing the flood – 1968

The offer to fish a private stretch of river usually conjures up in the mind a water full of fish bent on suicide, but it seldom works out that way. One does not turn down the chance to spend the day in such a place however and when the opportunity came my way, especially as the water was known to hold some big grayling, I jumped at the chance.

I received permission to fish on a private stretch of a York-shire river. The owner, who knows nothing about angling, said he knew there were grayling present, but had no idea of their size.

I left home with high hopes early one morning, just as the sky was beginning to lighten. As I had never seen the water concerned I planned on dumping my tackle and spending the first couple of hours examining the stretch, hoping I might spot some good fish and, if not, that I might sort out the most promising swims. Only another angler would appreciate my disappointment when, on arriving at the bridge that spans the river, I found the water fairly hurtling down in a brown spate. The alders which line the banks were standing in the river with the water three feet up their trunks.

I wandered disconsolately along the banks hoping to locate a quiet area where I might have some sort of chance, however remote, but the whole length (which is more or less straight) was one uniform piece of churning dirty water, which didn't offer a square foot that could be fished, with any sense. The wisest move would have been to cut my losses and return home but, after driving nearly eighty miles, I was determined to wet a line somehow.

To fish at all involved wading out to the alders in order to reach the river and this is what I did, aiming to fish a slightly less turbulent 'swim' close in to the boles of the trees. With so much free floating flotsam about, legering was out of the question. Several types of floats were tried and in the end I settled for a self-cocker which carried a single swan shot placed three feet above the hook, allowing the redworm bait to wander almost at will.

By mid-afternoon I had just convinced myself what a fool I was when the float, which was actually resting against the trunk of a tree, shot sideways into the current and I found myself struggling with what was obviously a good fish. It did almost as it pleased and took me longer to net than any I've ever hooked. I was using a 12ft hollow-glass roach rod which weighs 8½oz, a 2½lb line and a size 14 hook, and could only apply the lightest of pressure.

Once the fish gained the main push of water, which it did in about two seconds flat, there was little I could do except give line. I couldn't follow the fish, and the slightest check in such a cauldron would have meant an instant breakage.

It kept stopping momentarily, but as soon as contact was made, off it would shoot. On one occasion it moved across the stream and cruised upstream, parallel to the opposite bank. Quite suddenly, after a particularly long run – when I noticed how startlingly low the line appeared to be on the spool – the fish turned and began slowly moving towards me on my side of the river, close into the alders.

Until this moment I had seen no sign of the fish (in such a current it was impossible to tell exactly what I had hooked but deep down I was hoping it was a monstrous grayling!), but as I tightened gently on to it it leapt, showing itself to be a trout of fair proportions. In my disappointment I really laid on the pressure and duly landed an out-of-season, but well conditioned brown trout of over three pounds.

I decided to stick it out and fish until darkness. My legs were becoming stiff after standing all day up to my knees in water and there was barely enough light to see by when, for the second time, my float swung out into the current. This time I knew it was a grayling I had hooked and two minutes later a large sail-like fin showed on the surface. At 1½lb it was just half the weight I had wanted.

Perhaps one day I shall receive an invitation to return when I hope the water will be in better trim.

Nymph or maggot – 1968

My first outing that winter in search of grayling provided quantity but not quality. I finished the day with twenty fish and only four of them topped the pound mark. The day was cold and blustery with the river banks filled to the brim – you know the sort I mean, when the lapwings remained huddled on the stubble with their feathers blowing the wrong way and when the fingers are so numb it becomes a major effort to change a maggot.

It was a day when the grayling would have to be searched for in the quieter swims and encouraged to feed when found, at least that is what one would usually expect. But this time it was different. The steadier water running by slacks and lay-bys were unproductive and it was only when I tried the usual faster glides, which were moving like express trains, that results were obtained. Lesson one!

The second lesson, and one which I had feared, confirmed my theory that tiny spinners would sort out the better quality fish. This quickly came to light when I began to catch eight-inch grayling.

Although the water was high it wasn't coloured and I decided to settle down and float fish maggot or worm, but this time with a different set-up. It was a tip given me by a Lanarkshire angler, Charles Harrower, who claimed he had caught many big grayling with the method, especially in Scotland where he had taken several fish over 3lb. The idea is to fish a nymph on a four-inch dropper about two feet above the maggot. In a way you are getting the best of both worlds by covering fish which may be swimming at two different levels.

I caught twelve fish from that swim and all but one, including the four over one pound, came to the nymph. It doesn't always work and on occasions I have known it to work the other way round, but it's a useful extra method to have up your sleeve. I have trotted down artificial nymphs on both dropper and point, but for reasons I do not understand it doesn't work as well as when the nymph is used in conjunction with a maggot.

Conclusion

The grayling is a fish that has always fascinated me and still does to this day. During the winter months I usually have a few days fishing for them on the river Dove where the average weight is higher than the fish in its sister rivers, the Derwent, Wye and Manifold.

The fact that grayling survived from the ice age makes them an interesting fish to catch. It is this knowledge, linked with the fact that they will feed in temperatures much lower than other fish, that has brought about the misguided idea that they feed better when the river banks are gripped in frost.

A similar idea exists about pike – and still does in some circles – that they feed better during harsh winter conditions. Although both species will feed when the ice is forming in the margins, they will be much more responsive when the day is a mild one – or perhaps it would be more correct to say on a rising temperature.

During the early sixties I wrote an article in the angling

press which was titled 'Quest for a Three Pound Grayling'. Much to my surprise I received around two dozen letters suggesting where I might catch such a fish. Ninety per cent of them were in the same vein . . . 'there was one recorded here in 1902 (or some other date) weighing over three pounds', etc. What I was searching for was a river where the *average* weight was much higher than elsewhere. A few of the letters looked more hopeful and *all* the promising ones pointed to Scotland.

Following an exchange of letters it became apparent that the better-than-average fish were coming from rivers that had regular runs of salmon, and after some further probing I was left with the idea that there was a distinct possibility that these bigger fish might be waxing fat on salmon eggs.

It is my regret, and fault (!), that I never took up some of the invitations I was offered to fish these waters. I can only say that at the time I had become involved in chasing other species.

I still haven't caught my 3lb grayling. My best two fish to date, each weighing 2½lb, came from the Dove and the Driffield Canal in Yorkshire. I have hooked and lost what looked much bigger grayling on both waters, but I believe a three pound grayling is extremely rare, far more rare than a three pound roach.

It may surprise many grayling fishermen when I say that these days I seldom ever float or fly fish for grayling. It is several years ago since I realised that by far and away the best method to catch quantities of grayling was to leger for them. A light quiver-tip rod used in conjunction with a small swim feeder increased my catches dramatically, especially during times of high water. It is a case of wandering the banks until a fish is caught and then settling down to do battle.

Probably what surprised me most was the *lack* of sensitivity of the bites. It is all too easy to miss fish by striking too soon. Quite often the hook has to be retrieved with a disgorger. This seldom happens when float fishing.

I am sure, if you should drop among a shoal of fish that it is possible to catch every fish in the swim using this method. And there is no need to use hooks that are too small. I often use one of Drennan's size 14 eyed hooks tied direct to a three pound line.

TENCH – 1955

A week on the K.S.D.

I include the following piece, as it was written in 1955, since it records an important advance in the scale of match fishing that was taking place at the time. It was also a very interesting week's fishing for me.

The King Sedgemoor Drain which, until a few months ago, was comparatively unknown except to anglers in the south-west of England is now moving into first place and catching the eye of anglers throughout the length and breadth of the country. This coming September will see the banks of this quiet water lined with our expert matchmen competing for the honour of being England's number one champion.

As most anglers are aware, the 'All England' was designated to be fished on the Huntspill but as this river is not suitable to accommodate all the entrants, half of them will put their skill to the test on the K.S.D.

Last summer I spent a week fishing alone on the drain and a few words about it might be appreciated by contestants (of the forthcoming big match) and spectators alike. My intention on this visit was to improve my own tench record (the drain is renowned for its big tench) and I set my target at 5lb. I hooked two tench of at least that weight, of that I have no doubt but on the final day, of my five best fish over 2lb, the best weighed just under three. Not very impressive – only just over halfway to my target. Actually I had a very successful seven days and learned a lot which is of equal importance.

Before I illustrate briefly my experiences and results let me give you a quick insight into the species and average weights of fish contained in the drain at that time.

Tench: the average weight was high. Out of the many I caught the smallest turned the pointer of my spring balance to 1½lb. The local inhabitants showed no surprise whatsoever at my two pounders and everyone I talked to seemed to have caught fish of at least double that weight. The largest tench caught so far weighed 6lb 12oz.

Bream: these fish also had a high average weight – in the region of 3lb – odd 'grandfathers' of nearly 8lb occasionally coming to the net. As is peculiar to bream I found them swimming in shoals of similarly sized fish.

Roach: these were plentiful but not large and compared in size to the ones caught in matches fished on the Trent or Witham. The largest I caught, 12oz, somehow managed to swallow a lump of breadpaste intended for my specimen tench.

Along with perch, these were the fish which were liable to interest the matchmen. In recent years, carp had been introduced by the Bridgewater Angling Association but catches of these fish had been few and far between.

To return to my week. On the evening of the first day I spent an hour or so plumbing the depth (which seemed to average generally around 7ft in the middle) and choosing my spot into which, before I left, I deposited an ample supply of groundbait and choped worms.

Next morning, Sunday, I was there before the dawn 'cracked' and until breakfast time had a good mixed bag of bream and tench. I was using lobworms on a No 8 hook. The eels proved a nuisance (there were some whackers) so I decided that I would afterwards concentrate on paste or flake. Before leaving for my meal I threw in more ground-bait, together with a scattering of paste balls.

I would like to mention here that owing to the heavy rain-fall last summer the drain was almost continually being run off (Mr Porter, the water bailiff, informed me that had this not been so, sport would have been much better even than it was) and consequently I had to tackle up heavier than one would do normally. I started off by float-legering with a ½oz Arlesey bomb, but after the second day I discarded the float and in consequence caught more fish. The best results by far were obtained when the drain stopped being run off and I could remove the bomb and fish floatless and shot-less, the paste being easily cast to where I wanted it without any added weight.

After breakfast there was a lull for about two hours. I was idly chatting to a local farmer who was sitting behind me and wondering whether I ought not to fetch out the lobs again when my float, which was gently swaying in the pull of the water, started to show signs of animation and finally disappeared. I connected and knew I was on to something really good. 'It' hung fire for several minutes, just a dead weight cruising back and forth, a real heavy fish.

I was quite confident that I was master of the situation and that it was only a matter of time. The No 8 hook was tied direct to a new 5lb line. Suddenly, but without any mad dash, the fish turned its head towards Bridgewater Dock and set off. I lifted my finger from the spool to find that somehow the line had become firmly fast around the back.

My rod took on its battle-curve right down to the cork grip while I frantically scratched away trying to release the line. I had never seen the rod bend so much for a long time. Something had to go. Sidestrain was applied too late and with that awful, nauseating 'twang', the rod leapt back to its normal position. The new line had snapped above the float and I watched it, painfully mesmerised, as it slowly disappeared. I found it two days later 100 yards away in a weed bed with 15yd of line attached, minus the hook. In retrospect, I realise if I had dragged my idle body from its reedy couch and followed the fish along the bank I might, with a bit of luck, have reached my target!

On the Monday the sun shone brightly all day and as the tench seemed to be dozing I decided to try my hand at snatching roach, baiting with maggots. At the end of a few hours fishing I returned a 22lb mixed bag of roach, small bream and perch. For the remainder of the week I concentrated on tench, and together with bream had some very satisfying catches.

The climax came on Thursday morning at 7am when I hooked my second specimen. Twenty minutes later I had not even had a glimpse of it. Six yards to my right and extending about 8ft into the water were some tall reeds. The periodic attempts made by the fish to gain sanctuary therein were checked each time by sidestrain. At about its seventh attempt I was muttering 'No you don't, lad!' when I realised for a second time I had used sidestrain too late and he (or she) was in. All the necessary tricks of the trade were applied but I finally had to pull for a break and returned to my digs feeling somewhat dejected and late for breakfast.

To return to the big match. What effect hundreds of pounding gum-boots is going to have on those big tench I would not care to say but I will gamble there will be some grand catches of small stuff and someone is sure to drop among a shoal of bream. Given good weather conditions I would not be surprised if an all-time record is set up this year on the K.S.D.

140

Note: In fact both the individual and team weights turned out to be new records.

Margin fishing

An article by Norman Woodward in the *Angling Times*, discussing ways of taking good tench in the dark by fishing a bait close into the bank, prompted me to write this article. In case more anglers would care to try this method of catching not only tench but also bream and carp, I will describe the best manner I have yet found of using the tackle.

This style of angling, although neglected, was not new. I was using it successfully before the last war for catching bream, and it had been previously mentioned by other angling writers. The chief reason it is not more frequently pursued is that it is of no great value in daytime fishing, unless the banks are deserted, or the water is under flood conditions. The method is primarily for use during the night, and mainly for the catching of tench, carp and bream.

Lobworms are regarded by most anglers as a natural bait, i.e. one that fish are accustomed to finding in the water – not having been introduced by man. This observation when applied to enclosed waters is true, up to a point, but what we must realise is that it is not natural for lobworms to be found in the *centre* of lakes or ponds. Worms find their way into the water either by falling in off the bank, or being washed out of it during a period of heavy rain. They are discovered by the fish (naturally) *under* the bank, and never, at the most, more than a few feet from it.

Although hundreds of fish are caught on worms from the middle of the water, experience tells me that after dark, under certain conditions (warm night and fairly high water temperatures), a lob fished close in to the bank can be a killing bait.

The appropriate tackle designed for the handling of heavy fish should be used. I find a fixed spool reel ideal. The lob is cast parallel to the bank from the place one intends to sit and is allowed to fall close in to the side. It is seldom necessary to cast more than seven or eight yards. The water can be almost any depth down to about a foot or even less. No float is attached to the line, and only one shot is pinched on, about four feet from the hook, to ensure that the terminal tackle lies flat on the bottom.

The *two* rests are fixed so that when the rod is placed in them, it is pointing in the direction of the bait. After the slack has been taken up, the pick-up should be opened and a bite indicator attached to the line. I have the luxury of a 'buzzer', but a piece of silver paper is just as effective.

An alternative method of placing the bait is to drop it in the side where it is intended to lie, and then walk back to one's seat, paying off line from the spool at the same time. Casting should be cut down to a minimum, and the worm left undisturbed all night if necessary.

If you like to use two rods, as I often do, the second rod can be employed by margin fishing with a piece of crust floating directly under the rod point. If a fish is hooked on this second outfit, it is almost impossible for it to foul the other rod and line – which could happen if the bait on the first rod were lying farther out.

Quietness and good cover are essential to success when fishing at such short range and, of course, no lights must be shown or the fishing will be ruined. Fish come inshore after dark more than many anglers realise, sometimes feeding on the bottom, at other times on the surface. Whatever they are doing, 'bank lobbing' with one rod and crust fishing with the other can give us the best of two worlds.

First light and false hopes – 1962

How many times have you gone tench fishing for a week-end, dragged out a swim, baited up during the evening and fished from first light without getting results? Have you ever thought that it is possible to groundbait your swim too early? I had written in the past saying it was possible, on a soft-bottomed water, to drag out a swim too near to starting to fish. It is just as easy to mistime the hour that you should introduce your groundbait.

Many years ago my friend, Reg Brotherton, and I spent several weekends fishing a canal for tench. We used to arrive late Saturday afternoon or early evening and spend an hour or so dragging out a couple of swims, into which we deposited most of our groundbait. We would then fish until dark (usually with little success) at which time we would retire to our sleeping bags).

First light would find us full of hope and fishing assiduously at our baited swims. Sometimes we caught tench, often several tench, but more often than not we had to be satisfied with just an odd fish or two. We knew the water held a number of shoals of good tench, and these failures to make a large bag, under what were often ideal conditions, caused us much concern. I was convinced that we were at fault. Somewhere there was a slip-up in our methods, either in bait or tackle presentation, or we were fishing in the wrong place or at the wrong time.

On one occasion I thought I had solved the problem. The bottom was extremely soft, and I always had the uneasy feeling that most of the time we were fishing our baits were buried out of sight in the thick silt of the bed – although I was aware that *seriously* feeding tench would dig out an obscured bait with little difficulty. By changing to a piece of crust, so weighted to rest lightly on the bottom, I caught a few extra tench. But the success was only temporary; the problem hadn't been really solved.

It was when we were fishing a stretch where, through polaroid glasses, we could see the groundbait lying on the bottom that the truth finally dawned on us as to what was happening. On this particular visit we had carried out the same procedure – dragged a swim, deposited groundbait and fished until dark – with nothing to show. By peeping through the sedges we could see the groundbait nicely covering the centre of the swim.

The shock came the following morning when it became light enough to see into the water. The groundbait had disappeared; every single grain had vanished and the marauding tench that had filled their 'crops' during the hours of darkness were no longer present. They had moved on to pastures new.

Reg and I were not annoyed at this discovery: we were delighted. The problem that had dogged us for weeks had been solved. Subsequent visits to this and other waters have proved that it is possible to groundbait too soon. It is difficult to lay down any hard and fast rules as to how long before starting to fish one should bait up but during the summer months, if you intend fishing from first light, it is perhaps as well not to introduce your feed before midnight.

Fickle biting Tench need 'kidding' – 1966

There are times when tench will feed with such gay abandon that they can be caught by anyone. But there are other
occasions when each fish has to be worked for, and only the
man with a trick or two up his sleeve will catch tench.
We've all experienced days when tench are bubbling in the
swim but refuse to take a bait and at times I've often
remarked to a companion: 'I shall have to "kid" one out.'
This season I have been doing more tench fishing and more
'kidding' than usual.

I think that we sometimes have ourselves to blame for
finicky tench. In a freshly-cleaned swim, tench will often
become preoccupied with natural food disturbed by the
drag and completely ignore whatever is offered on the
hook. I am also convinced that tench can become pre-
occupied with groundbait and will feed on this to the
exclusion of other food items. It can be frustrating to say the
least, but all is not lost. There are several little dodges that
can be tried to get a fish to accept a bait.

If you suspect that tench are feeding on the groundbait,
then the first obvious trick is to use a bit of tightened-up
groundbait on the hook. Mix a piece of soft paste by using
less water, and use a lump big enough to cover at least a
size 10 hook.

The second bit of kidding you can apply is to try a
hookbait completely alien to the bait which has been
thrown in. Not long ago I laced a swim overnight with
maggots and at first light next morning the whole area was
alive with bubbling tench, but I couldn't catch them on
maggot hookbait! However, a change to a big lobworm on a
size 4 hook brought immediate response and I netted
several fine tench between 3lb and 4½lb.

I've brought about the same result in similar situations by
using a lump of paste or a large piece of flake; or sometimes
a dumpling – a combination of maggots on the bend and
paste on the hook shank.

It is really surprising how finicky tench can be, and it
pays continually to ring the changes until something accep-
table is discovered. If the swim has been baited with
coloured maggots it may be that the tench are picking up
only the pink ones or perhaps the yellow ones, so try that.

I know it helps to have the confidence of fishing with a

sensible hook, something between 10 and 4. But there are times when tench will only accept a single maggot or a piece of paste the size of a match head, and these should be tried on an eyed 16 hook. Care will have to be taken with a good fish – but first hook your tench.

The oldest trick I know of kidding out difficult tench is to drag the bait. All tench anglers will be familiar with the twitching float – when fish are toying with the bait, causing the float to do everything but submerge. The movements may cease after the first few preliminary bobs and then recommence after a short interval. The angler has no choice but to wait until the tench makes up its mind.

Sometimes the float will finally disappear but often the dithering stops when the bait is removed or the fish loses interest. Try moving the bait two or three inches when this happens. Such tactics can be fatal to hesitant tench. I don't know whether or not they imagine the bait is escaping and make a grab at it, but kidding tench this way frequently brings about their downfall.

Tenching with the Taylor brothers

In the late sixties, after a series of correspondence with Fred J. Taylor, I received an invitation to join them for a weekend tench fishing from one of their famous converted pontoons on Wooton Lakes.

Reg and I left Sheffield around midnight, both eagerly looking forward to our first meeting with the Taylor brothers. We made good time and, following Fred's instructions, arrived at the lakeside two hours before dawn.

As we didn't expect our hosts to arrive until dawn we spent a rather restless two hours in the car trying to get some sleep. When no one had turned up after three hours we decided to have a stroll round and look at the lake in daylight. Imagine our surprise when on reaching the boat house we found a note pinned to the door which read 'Tag, take the boat immediately behind you and row out to join us. We are on the pontoon'!

After introductions all round Fred put on the kettle and, as we drank a fresh mug of tea, he put us in the picture. He first apologised saying that they would have to leave us at 9am. Apparently they had forgotten about a local club match in which they all fished and this was the day. He also said the swims had been baited but the tench were not being as cooperative as usual. However, we caught a few fish and I remember catching a nice crucian of around 2lb but it became obvious it wasn't going to be a weekend of bulging keepnets.

But, my word, we did a lot of talking when Fred, Joe and Ken returned, and we enjoyed the experience of sleeping on the pontoon. A few more tench were caught on the Sunday morning until lunchtime when Reg and I had to pack our gear and return home.

EELS

This will be a short chapter! What can I say about eel fishing? I have taken part in several eel fishing sessions, but I have never enjoyed them. I never caught an eel above 2lb when doing the job properly, but I have caught a few three pounders plus when I have been fishing for other things.

My best came after dark when I was fishing an eight-inch deep, fast running stretch of river. I was legering a big lump of cheese for chub when the rod end gave a couple of dithers and then bowed over. Eels were the farthest thing from my mind and I was convinced I had hooked the grandfather of all chub, especially when it rolled, and in the darkness I had a vague glimpse of a white belly which looked nearly a yard long. It was terribly disappointing when I realised I was playing an eel. Even with my good sized landing net it was a devil of a job trying to net it from eight inches of fast water. It weighed 4½lb.

I know there are many enthusiastic eel anglers, and I have met a few, but I could never share their zest for the game. I always felt the time could be better spent chasing other species.

Sometimes I wonder whether I might have a subconscious fear of eels from the time when I first went fishing with my father in 1926. One day he caught an eel, the first I had ever seen, and as he was unhooking it I remember it wrapped itself around his forearm. I don't known how big it was but to my young eyes it seemed enormous. It is one of my earliest memories as a small child and the vision of my father struggling to unwind it has remained with me. It didn't help either when he cut off its head and it carried on trying to escape in the grass!

RUDD & CRUCIAN CARP

I would have liked to have done more fishing for both the above species, but there were few places within striking distance of home where they could be pursued.

My best crucian fishing, however, was on a small lake not too far from my house, but it was a private syndicate water and I was taken along as a guest on a few occasions by the late Eric Taylor.

We would meet at the water's edge at around 4.30am on a summer's morning and after fishing for four hours would both pack up in order that we could get into work by 9am. Sometimes we were a little late!

It was enjoyable fishing and we never failed to catch. The fish were of a high average weight and we caught few that were less than one pound. It was here I caught my best ever crucian of 2½lb. I wonder if they still average a good weight!

My rudd fishing has been very limited and my most exciting by far came when I was on an exercise in pursuit of carp. Jim Kirby was the fishing officer of the East Yorkshire branch of the Yorkshire Water Board. He rang me from his head office in Beverley to see whether I would try to catch a carp from a pond in his area. Apparently the water had been stocked some years earlier, but not a fish had been seen. I was due a week's holiday and I arranged with Jim to spend the last two days on the water.

The first two days of the week were spent after barbel on the river Swale and these were followed by two days fishing for tench at Drax pond near Selby. By the time I met Stan Metcalf, the River Board bailiff, who was to take me to the pond, I was feeling somewhat shattered. Much of the previous four days had been spent intensively fishing with hardly any sleep, and I was somewhat daunted as we stood on the banks and looked at a water that was covered from bank to bank in thick weed.

In my car I carried a home-made drag, which consisted of two sickle blades welded back to back onto a metal stem. I told Stan I would do my best and he left me to my task of trying to drag out some sort of a swim.

Two hours later, with a growing mountain of weed either side of me, the drag became fast on the bottom and pull as I might it remained solidly stuck. As I hadn't removed sufficient weed I had only one option left. Removing all my clothes, I half waded and half swam out, hanging on to the rope until I had passed the point where I judged the drag was embedded and gave it a good yank. The blades scythed up through the water nicking my leg *en route*.

However, after wrapping a handkerchief around a not too serious cut, I continued with my task and recall a little later dragging up, amongst the weed, a decomposed cow's head! After this gruesome discovery I called it a day and baited up with some mashed bread and scattered a few loose crusts on the surface. But after a long tiring night and a walk around the pond at dawn, I neither saw nor heard any sign of carp. Then, as the sun began to rise, I noticed the crusts being pushed around by some good sized rudd.

The carp never showed up the second night so I rigged out a more suitable tackle and had some exciting sport with rudd that weighed between one and nearly two pounds. I returned to the water a second time and took my best ever rudd of 2½lb.

The strange thing was that Jim never knew there were any rudd in the water and, as far as I know, there was never a carp caught from the pond. I often wonder whether Stan had taken me to the right water!

PERCH

Over the years I was often referred to by the angling press as being an 'expert' at catching carp, pike, barbel, chub, tench and grayling. In fact I never did concentrate on catching any one species long enough to be called an expert. I just went specimen hunting and reported my findings. What I was never labelled was a perch 'expert'.

I never did specialise for long at catching big perch, although I tried! Perch and grayling, it seemed to me, presented the same problems in that neither responded to the usual big fish tactics. A large bait would not sort out large perch from the average. As I mentioned earlier with grayling, I thought I had found a way of catching better quality fish by spinning for them with a small spoon, and I did catch some nice fish to over two pounds. But on subsequent trials I began to catch lesser fish – as little as four ounces – so I was back to where I started, and still am! I had similar experiences when I tried to sort out the bigger perch.

The first rule of specimen hunting, that of first find your fish, possibly applies more to perch than any other species. Perch do not grow big in every water, in fact they appear to demand certain habitat requirements that are not easy to define before they begin to slap on weight. It is strange how some waters produce millions of small nuisance perch but never seem to turn up a grandfather.

Water clarity seems to be essential, but what their food chain consists of I never discovered. In the fifties I used to fish one gin-clear water where the average size of the perch was around 1½lb. I caught over 30 on one occasion with not one fish under a pound in weight. All were taken on paternostered lobworm and were caught, in midsummer, in fifteen feet of water.

After several visits to this and several other waters over a space of four or five years I examined the stomach contents of perhaps three dozen perch. Only on two occasions did I find any sign of smaller fish, which were little perch. Various nymphs and other aquatic creatures appeared to make up the bulk of their diet.

150

I once caught some good perch between one and two pounds on floating casters! . . . husk, we used to call them. The fish were encouraged to feed by throwing in loose husks and then casting out one on light float tackle. A two pound plus perch on a size 16 hook puts up quite a show!

My best perch of just over three pounds was caught by accident when I was pike fishing and was just hauled out, weighed and returned. It had shot out from some rushes 'under my feet' and grabbed a three inch roach livebait I was retrieving.

In the late forties I caught a lot of perch, up to two pounds, by wandering along a canal using drop-minnow tackle. I doubt you could buy such gear today and would have to make your own. I suppose one could stuff a small lead-free bomb into the mouth of a dead minnow, tiny gudgeon or little roach. One point of a small treble is put through the lips of the bait (to prevent the bomb falling out) and a single eyed size 10 or 12 hook is stuck into the tail. Summer is the best time to wander along, dropping the bait into holes in the weedbeds. The rod is raised and lowered causing the dead-bait to rise and fall. Takes can usually be struck straight away.

The colour red is undoubtedly attractive to perch and if spinning with a tiny spinner I make sure the spoon has a bit of bright red wool attached to the treble.

Eary morning in summer (and possibly winter) is without doubt the best time to be out perch fishing. They are then at their most active. If I were to fish for them today I would certainly try fly tackle. There are some excellent artificial lures on the market which I am sure would be attractive to large perch.

Since starting to write this piece I have been out perch fishing on the middle reaches of the Derbyshire Derwent. I caught thirteen perch weighing a total of 26½lb. Amongst the haul were nine fish in excess of 2lb, with the best two weighing exactly 3lb each.

Here is an instance of first finding your fish, which I emphasised early on in the chapter. I was indebted to Andrew Henderson of Belper who did all the groundwork on these fish before inviting me to have a try for them. Andrew had taken several large perch from the same hole including two of 3lb 3oz. They were more or less confined to the one swim, and if fishing either side you were unlikely to catch more than just the occasional fish.

For many years I fished the river Idle without seeing a perch caught and then talked to an angler who had taken several big fish to over 4lb. He admitted that he had spent many fruitless hours searching until he finally found two spots where he caught perch fairly regularly.

TROUT

Although trout fishing has taken second place for much of my fishing life it has still formed an important part. I began trout fishing on a coarse fishing reservoir, Dam Flask, near Sheffield in the late forties.

It was an anything-goes-fishery and I amused myself by scattering floating maggot chrysalids on the surface and following them on the bank as they were pushed along by the breeze. Sometimes the trout would begin to rise at which time I would cast amongst them an imitative 'fly' that I had tied up with peacock herl.

I also spent some time fishing on small running waters that ran into, or out of, lakes and trout-holding reservoirs. I took trout from some of them weighing up to 2lb. Some of the streams were very tiny and in many places could be strode across, and from these little rivulets I caught a 'monster' of 1lb 10oz.

I introduced some members of the Cormorants AC to this style of fishing and many a happy hour was spent each Spring stalking along the banks. On one particular stream that ran through a wood it was truly delightful to wander along amidst flowering primroses and wood anemonies with both willow warblers and redstarts in full song.

It was often a hands and knees job, which was imperative for success, but it was great fun. The tackle was very simple: I used an eight foot fly rod and a small fixed spool reel loaded with two pound line. One shot was nipped on the line about six inches from a size 16 hook.

The idea was to creep upstream dropping the maggot baited hook into all the likely places. There were fish in nearly every small pool and if the approach had been careful enough then the sport could be fast and furious. On one visit I recall Reg Brotherton, Brian Thompson and myself catching and returning over seventy fish.

The tackle was altered slightly for the return journey, and about two feet up the line a one inch piece of tapered cork was secured with a matchstick. This was sent down a fast run into one of the numerous pools and it was exciting to watch it suddenly disappear as one of the game little 'brook' trout grabbed at the maggot.

When the reservoir vogue swung into fashion in the early seventies then this type of fishing began to take up more and more of my time. Bill Bartles and I teamed up and we made many trips to various reservoirs and trout waters up and down the country. Until Rutland opened its doors we did the long journey down the A1 to Grafham. It seemed an endless trip back after fishing all day until dark, and we were pleased when the massive reservoir at Rutland was opened for trout fishing. It meant about an hour less travelling either way, which made life a bit easier.

However, the increase in the cost of trout fishing, plus car expenses, put distant fisheries out of reach and I more and more turned to Ladybower reservoir in Derbyshire. It is here I now spend most of the summer season and it is from this magnificent water that I have taken some of my best trout catches including my best ever rainbow. This fish weighing 11lb 14oz turned out to be the best fish of the 1991 season from the reservoir and, as well as earning me a 'Troutmaster' badge, also qualified me for the final competition fished in May 1992. In July 1993 I also caught my best brown from Ladybower: a splendid trout weighing 9½lb.

SEATROUT

If I were asked to say what was my very favourite sort of fishing, I would probably have to admit that it was fly fishing for seatrout after dark. There is little doubt that had there been such fishing nearer home then I would have done far less fishing for other species.

As most carp anglers will testify, there is something magic about fishing during the dark hours . . . or perhaps these days they sleep in a bivvy! To be by, or usually in, a seatrout river at night casting a fly into the darkness, with the current pushing against your waders, waiting for that unbelievable tug on the line is something more than just magic.

The occasional fish to around 2lb had been picked up accidentally when I had fished for grayling on the Yorkshire Esk, but it was during the late sixties/early seventies that I really fished for seatrout properly. It was then, after finishing work on a Friday, that Reg Brotherton and I would motor across to Bedgellert in North Wales to spend either one or two nights fishing the river Conway. Irrespective of water conditions we bought our ticket at a local hotel and went down to the river.

Only on one occasion were we unable to fish and this was because we arrived in mid-June and the hotelier said they didn't start selling tickets until July! Not wishing to return home after such a long trip, I remember we drove up a long winding track high into the mountains until we reached a lake that was supposed to hold trout. We slept under the stars in the heather and began fishing at first light, but we caught only a few small fish.

On three different visits I fished the river on my own and in retrospect it was not a wise thing to do. The first trip still haunts me to this day. I had driven across in steady rain and on arrival was surprised to find the water was uncoloured and only a little above normal height. It was still raining and, after tackling up, I donned my chest waders and sat in the little fishing hut sipping coffee and awaiting darkness.

It was still pouring as I waded out to my favourite spot

and twenty minutes later I netted my first fish of 2½lb. After taking it ashore I returned to my pitch and after twenty minutes I had a wonderful tussle with another fish which weighed just over 5lb. This, I mused, was going to be my night! The late Cyril Inwood had fished in exactly the same spot where I was standing and he had taken several fish in excess of ten pounds.

More than an hour later the rain was still coming down in typical Welsh fashion but I was unperturbed, even when I realised I was having to lean a bit harder against the push of the current. The night was really black and at some point I glanced down to check the water level on my waders. At this place in the river I knew the water at normal height was about eight inches below the top. I noticed with horror that it was just lapping the brim and at the same moment a branch, floating down on the surface, hit me in the back.

Teetering on my toes for a few seconds I fought against a rising panic. As I turned in the pitch blackness I couldn't even see the silhouettes of the trees on the bank and for a little while wasn't exactly sure I was moving in the right direction. However, the water around my chest began to drop and it was a great relief when I finally stumbled up the bank. But I hadn't learned my lesson!

On another trip when fishing by myself I thought it would increase my chances if I could get to the other side where some big fish were splashing under the opposite bank. There were some shallows downstream where the river widened and with rod and landing net I set off to cross just after midnight. The water was more fierce than I had thought and it took a long time to pick my way carefully across in the darkness. *En route* I made up my mind that I would fish until dawn so that I could return in daylight.

I must have covered nine tenths of the journey when I reached what proved to be a fast, deep, un-fordable gully. It was an awful thought, as I looked upstream at the white water bearing down on me, that I had to re-trace my steps. Such tactics are stupid. One should never carry out such manoeuvres alone on a river at night.

There was another trip, less dangerous but never-the-less memorable, when I arrived early at the water and instead of waiting until darkness to begin fishing I rigged up a small spoon and decided to do a bit of spinning. Across the river in a deep run were several large seatrout

156

and I couldn't resist the temptation to try for one. They were not easy to catch during the day and when I pulled into a heavy fish I thought it must be a salmon. I was using my carp rod matched to an 11lb line and was full of confidence.

Thinking I would show this fish what such a combination of rod and line could do, I laid into it very hard. I checked every run and bullied it upstream in double quick time until I had it thrashing in front of me in some shallow water. It was then I realised that it wasn't a salmon but a huge, lovely conditioned seatrout that was well into double figures. At this point of realisation the spinner left its jaws and flew past my head like a rocket and I watched, mesmerised, as a very surprised fish rolled over and returned to the deeps.

SALMON

A 'salmon fishing expert' is something I have never been called, but I must admit that whenever I have fished for them the experience has been very enjoyable.

In England I have fished for them on the Lune in the company of a true expert, Arthur Oglesby, from whom I learned a lot. In Scotland I have tried several rivers including the Spey, Tummel, Tay and the Spean; all of them with various degrees of success.

The most exciting by far was when fishing the Spean at Gairlochy. A farmer friend gave me permission and I fished his stretch on several occasions. The approach was perhaps as exciting as the fishing and when I first saw the water I understood what he meant when he suggested that catching salmon there was a two man job.

Anyone familiar with the Spean will know that in places the river tumbles fiercely through high sided gorges. The first part of the 'assault course' was in getting down to the river with the aid of a rope that was left permanently in position. Once this hazard had been negotiated with tackle, bait, etc, one then arrived on some massive boulders with the river rushing past twelve feet below.

On my first visit I went alone and lost two fish because I couldn't get down to the water to gaff them. On subsequent trips I was accompanied by my wife who bravely climbed down the rope. After hooking a fish I would play it until it was completely exhausted, when the rod would be passed to my wife while I gingerly eased my way to the water down a narrow gully with the gaff. The dangers can be imagined; one slip and there would be no return!

The river tore through this confined gorge and spilled out through a small entrance into a pool. Fish were caught either by spinning upstream in the fast water or by bait fishing in the pool. When upstream spinning every hooked fish took the same evasive action. It shot past one downstream, through the narrow 'gut' and into the pool where, if it hadn't come unstuck, it had to be played out. On first contact the rod had to be held high to avoid the line cutting on the rocks while one followed over a second obstacle course trying to keep in touch.

The largest fish I caught there weighed only 11lb, which is perhaps as well because there was the task of getting it back, together with one's gear, up the rope. I never landed more than two on any one occasion and this involved the nightmare of two journeys!

I hope to do more salmon fishing whenever the opportunity occurs, but I might give the Spean a miss!

SEA FISHING

What can I write about sea fishing? Not a lot! It was mostly carried out on family holidays and, to be honest, I never learned to understand it, although I did manage to capture a few good fish. I was a fool when it came to working out tides and consequently was seldom in the right place at the right time! I did seem to catch more than my fair share of crabs!

I could never come to terms with the, often necessary, heavy tackle that had to be used much of the time. Fishing for codling from rocks and casting into kelp beds using fifty or sixty pound breaking strain line was far removed from the fishing I understood.

I have many friends who are sea anglers and they have my greatest respect, certainly the ones who shorefish on a winter's night in the face of a north-easterly!

Once I had a passion to catch a bass and on a week's holiday on the Lynn peninsular in North Wales my family suffered while I went, unsuccessfully, through the motions. I fished on the right beach, both by day and by night, but I never saw a bass. Eventually, on another holiday and under the guidance of that great sea fisherman, Bruce Macmillan, I fished early one morning in the Menai Straights and managed to catch two bass weighing around 3lb each. I should have caught more but I had misjudged the tide!

I also boat fished with Bruce off the Welsh coast and caught a 32lb tope and a thornback ray. I didn't enjoy catching either fish. As I was playing the tope I was being sea sick over the side!

Perhaps the sea fishing I enjoyed most was spinning for mackerel off Filey Brigg or the North shore at Scarborough using a small spoon and a light spinning rod. I must try and fit in another session next summer.